*the*
# 10 Best
## Kentucky Derbies

## Also Available from Eclipse Press

# *the* 10 Best Kentucky Derbies

By the Staff and Correspondents of

## The Blood-Horse

RACING'S LEADING WEEKLY PUBLICATION

FOREWORD BY D. WAYNE LUKAS

ECLIPSE
PRESS

Essex, Connecticut

An imprint of Globe Pequot, the trade division of
The Rowman & Littlefield Publishing Group, Inc.
4501 Forbes Blvd., Ste. 200
Lanham, MD 20706
www.rowman.com

Distributed by NATIONAL BOOK NETWORK

British Library Cataloguing in Publication Information available

**Library of Congress Cataloging-in-Publication Data available**

LCCN: 2004113515

ISBN 9781581501186 (cloth)
ISBN 9781493073337 (paperback)
ISBN 9781493079438 (epub)

♾™ The paper used in this publication meets the minimum requirements of
American National Standard for Information Sciences—Permanence of Paper for
Printed Library Materials, ANSI/NISO Z39.48-1992.

# Contents

# Foreword

YOU'RE NEVER REALLY PREPARED for the way it affects you and the feelings you experience. The emotion just kind of sweeps over you like the dense fog on some of those damp Saratoga mornings. And then it hits you full force as over a hundred thousand strong raise their voices in that familiar refrain: "Weep no more, my lady." And even if you've been there before, you still lose a little bit of your composure. You try to remain calm, and yet when the horses step onto the track and they strike up "My Old Kentucky Home," it's hard to keep your emotions in check.

The tradition and impact of the Kentucky Derby comes full circle at that moment.

Of the forty thousand-plus foals born each year, only some fifteen to twenty will approach the Churchill Downs starting gate on the first Saturday in May with a chance at Derby glory. Each and every one of us who has ever trained a horse has looked at every yearling and hoped that he or she would be the one. The beautiful part about the Kentucky Derby is that each year somebody is going to experience the ultimate thrill in horse racing.

As you watch the horses go to the post, your mind flashes back to two short years ago when you first saw the marvelous three-year-old colt or filly that now bears your handiwork and the hopes and dreams of its owners. You have spent the last two years nurturing the young horse, pulling, pushing, prodding, to bring its talent to the fore, knowing that on this day everything has to come together and that your horse has only two minutes to take its place among the other greats.

No matter how many times you have witnessed the Kentucky Derby post parade, nothing can lessen the impact. You're no less

involved, and in most cases your emotions run even higher because you have experienced it before. You reach the pinnacle of your profession when you win the Derby. For me, each time has been unique, whether it was entering the winner's circle with the filly Winning Colors, winning with longshots Thunder Gulch and Charismatic, or standing next to my best friend, W.T. Young, wondering if Grindstone had nosed out Cavonnier.

I've always felt that the Kentucky Derby seemed to reward people in our industry for meritorious service. If you look back through the history of the Derby and its 131 years, the names of the people connected to the winners parallel and ring true to those individuals who have meant so much to the sport. You look down through the roster with Calumet and the Wrights, Paul Mellon, the Hancock family, the Chenerys, W.T. Young, and Robert and Beverly Lewis, and it seems like the gods of racing have smiled on these people on this particular day to reward them for the way they have carried the sport.

Now, Blood-Horse Publications and Eclipse Press, through an extraordinarily talented and gifted group of writers, bring you *The 10 Best Kentucky Derbies*. Obviously, the ten best are a matter of opinion, and certainly the ten in this book are debatable because everyone has his or her favorite Derby. In *The 10 Best Kentucky Derbies*, these writers take you behind the scenes, onto the backside, and into the barns and let you become a first-hand observer in what went into the making of these memorable events.

For each and every special Derby — and they're all special — there are some wonderful stories that many people never have the opportunity to hear. These are stories that sometimes are so improbable, so irresistible, or so fitting that even the best Hollywood scriptwriters could not equal their drama and excitement.

The sun shines bright on my old Kentucky home.

*D. Wayne Lukas*
*Four-time Derby winner, Hall of Fame*

# Introduction

LEGENDARY TURF WRITER JOE HIRSCH once said he never met a Kentucky Derby he didn't like. I couldn't agree more. Yet each person takes home a different Derby memory. Some memories are more special than others, and those are the ones you keep a little closer to the heart.

There are no set criteria in determining the most memorable Derbies. They can be Cinderella stories such as the unlikely tales of Black Gold and Canonero II. They can be dramatic, controversial stretch runs like the one between Brokers Tip and Head Play and the one between Iron Liege and Gallant Man, or even the near-disastrous stumble by Alysheba and his remarkable recovery. And they can be bravura performances, such as those turned in by Secretariat and Whirlaway.

They could have nothing to do with the actual running of the race or the winner. The eagerly anticipated showdowns between Affirmed and Alydar and between Citation and Coaltown made those respective Derbies unforgettable to those who were around to experience them. And finally, they can be ground-breaking, such as the victory by the filly Regret and the post-race comment heard 'round the racing world by her distinguished owner, Harry Payne Whitney.

These are the ten stories that await the reader, along with a kaleidoscope of vibrant images only the Kentucky Derby can produce. A panel of five that includes yours truly ranked these epic sagas as the ten best Derbies for a special issue of *The Blood-Horse* magazine in 2000. That ranking provided the genesis for this book, and the recounting of these Derbies by a diverse group of Turf writers will transport

the reader to Louisville, Kentucky, on the first Saturday in May.

With a history as rich as the Derby's, it wasn't easy to narrow the list to ten. How can you leave out the great stretch battle and budding rivalry between racing's undefeated golden boy, Majestic Prince, and the gallant Arts and Letters? For sheer brilliance, you can't get much better than Spend a Buck, who blew the 1985 Derby wide open against one of the deepest fields ever assembled. And in the process, he changed the face of the Triple Crown by passing the Preakness to go for a $2-million bonus in the Jersey Derby, thus initiating the $5-million Triple Crown bonus that still waits to be won after nearly twenty years.

You also had the controversial stretch battle between Tomy Lee and Sword Dancer; the shocking upset of Native Dancer by Dark Star; and the upset of all upsets by 91-1 shot Donerail. Perhaps they too will come alive again in future Derby books.

But the ten chosen by panelists Joe Hirsch, Jim McKay, Bob Adair, Mike Battaglia, and me provide a vast tapestry of the Kentucky Derby, while profiling some of the most gifted athletes and colorful characters in the history of the sport.

So, curl up in your favorite chair with a mint julep and a dozen roses, and as you travel through the pages of Derby lore, take a sip of the julep and a whiff of the roses and envision the famed Twin Spires piercing a bright cerulean sky on the first Saturday in May. It's called Derby Fever. Catch it.

*Steve Haskin*
*Hamilton Square, New Jersey, 2004*

# The Legend of Big Red

## (Secretariat, 1973)

FOR MONTHS HE HAD BEEN SIMPLY BRILLIANT. Everything about him, from his looks to his attitude to his competitive fire, stood him apart. Experts struggled to describe him suitably, often evoking past greats for comparison, while fans of all ages marveled at his dominance. He was causing waves of excitement on a global scale. No horse, at least none in recent memory, had managed to attract such widespread attention.

Suddenly all of it was in question. Only days shy of the most important assignment of his young life — the ninety-ninth Kentucky Derby — he had been soundly defeated. His race had been uninspiring. He had looked dull. For the first time ever Secretariat appeared vulnerable.

Now there was a great sense of urgency, for much more than just a reputation would be at stake. Millions of dollars, supplied by magnates throughout the world, had already been poured into the colt's future as a stallion, and his loss had left many investors in a panic. Another failure and his value would begin to plummet. For Secretariat and his closest supporters, victory in the Derby was an absolute must. Everything was on the line.

In terms of sheer drama the 1973 renewal of the Kentucky Derby is still hard to top. Secretariat's bid to capture the nation's preeminent horse race was steeped in action and emotion, romance and suspense. At its core, though, was the element of redemption. When Secretariat came flying down the stretch that sunny Saturday afternoon, his chest-

A jubilant Penny Chenery and Ron Turcotte lead Secretariat to the winner's circle

BOB COGLIANESE

nut coat forever emblazoned in the minds of racegoers young and old, all the rumors, the uncertainty, and the angst were put to rest. The son of Bold Ruler had indeed restored his standing as the best three-year-old around, and he did it by running the Kentucky Derby faster than any other horse in history.

Secretariat's unparalleled performance in the Derby served as a powerful preamble to his sweep of the '73 Triple Crown, an accomplishment considered by many to be the greatest that Thoroughbred racing has ever seen. Since 1896, when Ben Brush took the first Kentucky Derby ever contested at a mile and a quarter, no winner had managed to complete the race in less than two minutes. Decidedly got close in 1962, as did '67 winner Proud Clarion and even Northern Dancer, whose time of 2:00 flat in 1964 stood as the Derby standard for nearly a decade.

Secretariat came along and promptly blew the two-minute barrier to bits. His final time, 1:59 2/5, remains the benchmark for others to surpass, and since then only one horse — 2001 victor Monarchos — has approached his record. What distinguishes Secretariat's Derby from all others, however, is the manner in which he won. It is a given that Thoroughbreds, when competing at such a distance, gradually slow as the race evolves. Secretariat's achievement defied that law. His was a run of pure acceleration, a continuous increase in speed that had him traveling his fastest as the Derby drew to a close. More amazing was that he did it largely on his own, receiving just token urging from his rider, Ron Turcotte.

But that was only part of the story.

It would be difficult to imagine another horse arriving at Churchill Downs attended by as much hoopla as Secretariat was in 1973. Even as a two-year-old, several months before his historic effort in the Kentucky Derby, he was a source of captivation. As a physical specimen, Secretariat had a muscular build that belied his youth. As an athlete, he moved with breathtaking style, combining the raw power of a fullback with the agility of an Olympic gymnast. Few could match his ability to quicken, and despite his age, he handled adversity with the air of a veteran.

THE BLOOD-HORSE PHOTOS

Secretariat (opposite) poses as photographers shuffle to get the perfect winner's circle shot; (Inset) The Chenery family, trainer Lucien Laurin (second from left), and jockey Ron Turcotte enjoy the trophy presentation

His races generated much intrigue. Throughout the summer and fall of 1972, Secretariat delivered one knockout after another for Turcotte, owner Penny Chenery, and the colt's trainer, Lucien Laurin. The powerful chestnut piled up a slew of stakes at Saratoga, Belmont, Laurel, and Garden State, and in the minds of many — including those in press boxes around the country — he was the single most dynamic Thoroughbred to compete that year. Not even his disqualification from a rousing win in Belmont's Champagne Stakes could sully their opinions. That winter Secretariat became the first two-year-old ever to be named undisputed Horse of the Year.

The fascination only ballooned from there. Within weeks of his championship, it was announced that the colt had been syndicated for stud duty, and upon the conclusion of his three-year-old season, he would retire to Claiborne Farm near Paris, Kentucky — the home of his late sire, Bold Ruler — to begin his own career as a stallion. Given his potential for greatness beyond the track, Secretariat resembled a new issue stock, attracting interest from around the globe. Industry moguls, prominent breeders, and businessmen throughout North America, plus some far-reaching individuals from England, Ireland, France, and Japan, had pitched in to purchase a piece of the future. Their gamble, at $190,000 a share, made Secretariat the most expensive sire prospect in the history of Thoroughbred breeding. When the dust had finally settled in early '73, his price had hit $6,080,000, a world record.

"You've always heard that statement, 'He's worth his weight in gold,'" William Nack, author of *Secretariat: The Making of a Champion*, remarked. "He was literally worth three times his weight in gold."

This unprecedented syndication, following on the heels of Secretariat's spectacular '72 season, prompted sensations throughout the sport. From casual fans to insiders, expectations for Secretariat were considerable. He was viewed as a messiah, a colt of preternatural talent, the one with the best chance to bring Thoroughbred racing its first Triple Crown in a quarter of a century. Nevertheless, as the new year dawned, Secretariat still had something to prove.

"In my heart it was questionable whether this was something he was destined to do or not," Chenery recalled. "I was always aware that he could be the flashy two-year-old who does not pan out as a three-year-old. His style of racing was so explosive that he might not be able to stretch it out to the classic distance. He pounded the ground, and he was very heavy-headed. It sounds naïve to say, but I felt he was in danger of just shaking himself apart. It was always in the back of my mind."

Secretariat's lineage, too, fueled some additional speculation. In the modern era no other stallion had so dominated American breeding and racing as Bold Ruler did during the 1960s and early '70s. A son of the illustrious Nasrullah, Bold Ruler had overcome a litany of physical setbacks to stamp himself as one of his generation's finest runners. He was a colt of tremendous will, for despite his infirmities he competed in many of the nation's top races, setting track records and carrying hefty imposts at an array of distances. In 1957 Bold Ruler won the Preakness Stakes and was later named Horse of the Year.

His impact at stud, however, far exceeded anything he had ever accomplished on the track. Starting in 1963, he was the foremost stallion in North America for seven successive years, a reign that has not been duplicated since. During that span he produced a host of stakes winners, several of whom became champions. By the end of 1972, well after his son Secretariat had first made headlines, Bold Ruler's offspring had amassed more than $14 million in purse earnings, a figure never before attained by a Thoroughbred sire anywhere. He was, in short, phenomenal.

"All those Bold Rulers could run. Every one of them," Hall of Fame jockey Laffit Pincay Jr. remembered. "If you had a Bold Ruler, you had something good."

But Bold Ruler was not impervious to scrutiny, and according to several pundits, his presence in Thoroughbred bloodlines was not only an advantage but also a liability. Despite the stallion's profound success in the breeding shed, conventional wisdom held that his progeny lacked overall stamina, that they became less and less effective as race distances lengthened. There were, naturally, exceptions to this rule.

Bold Ruler's champion daughters Lamb Chop and Gamely each captured important ten-furlong stakes as three-year-olds and won numerous times at nine furlongs. The gifted Reviewer, plagued by injuries like his sire, once held the track mark for one and one-eighth miles at Belmont. Another son, Bold Bidder, took the mile and a quarter Charles H. Strub Stakes at age four, establishing a new Santa Anita record in the process.

KINETIC CORP.

**Secretariat leads the post parade for the ninety-ninth Kentucky Derby**

In large part, though, the theory held water. For every Lamb Chop and Gamely there were many like Queen Empress and Queen of the Stage, both champion two-year-old fillies who failed miserably in races longer than one and one-sixteenth miles. For every Reviewer there were several like Vitriolic, the country's top juvenile male of 1967, who was a flop the following year. And for every Bold Bidder there were others like Bold Lad, a one-time champion and the beaten favorite in the 1965 Kentucky Derby, who lost every time he ran beyond a mile.

"A lot of the Bold Rulers were like Bold Lad," Nack explained. "They showed a lot of speed at two and then they fizzled."

Bold Ruler had been putting up baroque numbers for years, and no other stallion around could match his stats. But one unavoidable fact remained: For all his worth he had yet to father a winner of the Kentucky Derby, Preakness, or Belmont Stakes. From all angles, however, Secretariat outshone his Bold Ruler brethren. On sheer talent he was clearly the best of the entire bunch. If any horse seemed bound to dispel these knocks, Secretariat was the one.

Anticipation for his seasonal debut was understandably high, and his return to action finally came in March, when he met five rivals in Aqueduct's Bay Shore Stakes. At seven furlongs the Bay Shore presented an ideal kickoff to his three-year-old campaign. It was also his first race in nearly four months. Secretariat, though, looked like he had never skipped a beat. Surging through traffic in early stretch, he won by four and a half lengths. The quest for the Kentucky Derby was on.

If Secretariat's win in the Bay Shore seemed impressive, his effort in the Gotham Stakes three weeks later was flat-out awesome. With the field moving up the backstretch in the one-mile Gotham, Turcotte, in a deviation from his customary tactics, put Secretariat on the lead. The chestnut colt motored around the far turn, shook off a single challenger racing for home, and crossed the line three lengths clear. After a six-furlong split of 1:08 3/5 — a time sure to win most top-level sprints — Secretariat finished in 1:33 2/5, matching the Aqueduct track record.

There was added luster to his victory. As he had in the Bay Shore, Secretariat took the Gotham under 126 pounds, the same weight he

would be asked to handle throughout the Triple Crown. More important, clockers had closely followed him as he continued past the wire, and what they observed left them in disbelief. While Secretariat gradually decelerated, galloping out around the clubhouse turn, his momentum carried him an extra quarter-mile in twenty-six seconds. He had thus traveled a mile and a quarter in less than two minutes, faster than Northern Dancer's existing record for the Kentucky Derby.

The implications of such a feat were obvious. It was not the first occasion, though, that his speed had caused a stir. Fast times would forever be part of the Secretariat mystique. As a two-year-old, he had won the Hopeful Stakes at Saratoga and then the Belmont Futurity — each contested at six and a half furlongs — and had come perilously close to setting track records in both races. Were it not for an October downpour in Maryland, he most certainly would have broken the course mark for one and one-sixteenth miles in the Laurel Futurity. As

THE BLOOD-HORSE

**Secretariat bounds home in front of Sham to win in track-record time**

it was, he missed by a fifth of a second.

Even his workouts became the stuff of trackside conversations. Secretariat was known to turn in blazing drills during training, and the faster he worked in the morning, the better he performed in the afternoon. Three days before the Bay Shore, for example, he scorched three furlongs at Belmont in :32 3/5, finishing out the half-mile in :44 4/5. In preparation for the Gotham, he knocked off a mile in a racy 1:35 2/5. The trend would carry on throughout his career. Such routine exertion would have caused horses of lesser quality, especially young ones, to crumble. For Secretariat the heavy regimen was vital.

"He thrived on it, and if you didn't give him a hard workout before the race, he didn't do as well. It was what he needed," Chenery explained. "You couldn't give Secretariat too much work. Lucien was the perfect trainer for him because he wasn't afraid to tighten the screws, and the horse could take it. A different trainer might not have gotten the best out of Secretariat. He really knew how to crank up a horse."

"The key to Secretariat was to blow him out on the eve of a race," Nack noted. "I'd seen him run off of great workouts and I'd seen him run off of bad workouts. It was night and day with him. This horse needed fast workouts."

By the spring of '73, Secretariat was roundly regarded as a superstar. He had been multidimensional, showing the ability to take command of a race at virtually any point. He could withstand pressure, displaying poise when faced with bad bumps, heavy weights, sloppy tracks, or tight quarters. He had racked up one stakes win after another, ranging in distances from six furlongs to one and one-sixteenth miles, and none of the outcomes had been remotely close. His speed and finishing kick had been impossible for anybody to counter. Compared to his competition, Secretariat was an entirely different breed of athlete.

With one shocking defeat, however, things nearly unraveled.

"If you look at the Wood Memorial on television after you've seen the Bay Shore, the Gotham, and then the Derby, he's like a different animal," explained Nack. "He was doubly condemned going into the Wood, and

he was running against the best racehorse he'd ever run against. No horse was considered a factor against Secretariat like Sham."

Secretariat's status as the country's main Kentucky Derby contender was intact even before the year got underway. Sham, on the other hand, began 1973 as a virtual nobody. Within a matter of weeks, though, he had surfaced as the best three-year-old colt on the West Coast. His pedigree and physique, combined with ample talent, made him a prime candidate to withstand the Triple Crown crucible.

Brawny in build and powerful in movement, Sham was among the first crop of runners sired by Kentucky stallion Pretense. As a racehorse, Pretense had shown few limits. His inherent speed had led him to a number of stakes wins sprinting. His stamina had earned him victories in both the Santa Anita and Gulfstream Park handicaps, two of the most prestigious distance events in the nation. His versatility had enabled him to excel on the turf, where he once established an American record at one and one-sixteenth miles. His son Sham seemed sure to make him a household name at stud.

The horse had a world of potential. Though Sham began his career winning just one of four starts as a two-year-old, he flourished when his trainer, Frank "Pancho" Martin, took him from New York to southern California for the winter. Fiery and outspoken, Martin was convinced he had a first-rate prospect on his hands, and the dark bay colt soon lived up to the billing. Sham made a meal out of his competition out west, and a clear-cut triumph in the mile and one-eighth Santa Anita Derby drew raves from far and wide. Those with educated eyes could tell that Sham would definitely present an obstacle for Secretariat.

A confrontation between the two was certain to take place five weeks hence at Churchill Downs. Martin, however, was keen to test the champ right away, so he shipped Sham back to New York to take on Secretariat in Aqueduct's Wood Memorial. It shaped up as a showdown, the perfect appetizer for the upcoming Triple Crown contests. Instead, the Wood was a topsy-turvy affair, although Sham did emerge from the race with his reputation more or less unblemished. For

Secretariat and his connections, the result of the Wood could not have been much worse.

Secretariat's failure stemmed largely from inadequate fitness. Leading up to the Wood, circumstances prevented Secretariat from training with his typical vigor. The pivotal workout came four days beforehand, when he logged a lackluster mile at Belmont in 1:42 3/5, several seconds slower than planned. It left him woefully unprepared to meet a horse of Sham's caliber, especially going nine furlongs. Compounding matters was an infected abscess in Secretariat's mouth. Roughly the size of a silver dollar, it was located beneath his upper lip and discovered by a veterinarian just hours before the race. The abscess was terribly sensitive, too, creating much pain whenever Turcotte applied pressure to the colt's bit. Only Laurin and Secretariat's groom, Eddie Sweat, were made aware of it.

"Had I had any knowledge of it, I would have ridden him differently," said Turcotte, remembering Secretariat's uncharacteristic behavior as the Wood unfolded. "Every time I picked his head up, he just threw it in my face. He just didn't want any part of that. I had no idea what was happening or what was wrong."

While Turcotte struggled with Secretariat on the track, thousands more in the Aqueduct grandstand were swathed in confusion. They had seen Angle Light, Secretariat's unsung stablemate, lead the Wood from start to finish, unsettling the entire three-year-old division. They had seen Sham whittle away at Angle Light down the stretch, only to lose by a head. And they had seen Secretariat, lacking his usual oomph, laboring just to be third, and looking terrible in the longest race of his life. None of it made any sense.

"I watched in disbelief also. I couldn't understand it," admitted Chenery. "But having him beat in the Wood did take off some pressure. Then we knew that he was fallible, so the Derby would be a real race and not a coronation. In a sense, it was easier for me."

It was not the first time that Chenery had been exposed to the vagaries of the Kentucky Derby trail. The Meadow, the Chenery family's breeding and racing operation in Virginia, had sent four other colts

to Churchill Downs before Secretariat. Situated on approximately 2,600 acres of lush landscape near Richmond, The Meadow was founded in 1936 by Chenery's father, Christopher, when he purchased and began to restore land that had belonged to the family since before the Civil War. A renowned industrialist, Christopher Chenery had invested profusely in his new acquisition, eventually transforming the once-neglected terrain into a haven for nurturing young Thoroughbreds. One of them, the filly Hildene, would end up producing the farm's first two champions, Hill Prince and First Landing.

Through the years Penny Chenery had been distantly involved with The Meadow, but she had witnessed firsthand its run of disappointment in Louisville. Hill Prince had been the nation's top two-year-old colt of 1949 and the next spring became the stable's first starter in the Kentucky Derby. He ran second, beaten just over a length by Middleground. First Landing had followed a similar path, finishing third behind Tomy Lee and Sword Dancer in 1959. The cruelest blow, however, had come in 1962, when the talented Sir Gaylord carried The Meadow's hopes right up to the race, broke down during training, and never ran again.

It would be a full decade before the family would return. By 1972 Christopher Chenery was in failing health, and Penny, his youngest child, had assumed the responsibility of overseeing The Meadow's progress. At the time, the leader among the farm's runners was three-year-old Riva Ridge. He was a homebred son of First Landing and, like his sire before him, had earned a championship as the best juvenile colt in the country. Riva Ridge had continued to improve into the spring, and his commanding victory in the Blue Grass Stakes at Keeneland made him the heavy favorite to win the ninety-eighth Kentucky Derby. Despite the public's confidence in Riva Ridge, Chenery's previous letdowns at the Derby had taught her to maintain a great deal of personal restraint.

"I tried never to get too high, and I tried never to make any assumptions. I just didn't let myself get too excited," she said. "I did not expect to win with Riva, but I was hopeful, so when he did win, it was just a

THE COURIER-JOURNAL

**Penny Chenery rejoices after Secretariat's victory**

great thrill. I thought that I had lived out my father's greatest goal, we'd done it during his lifetime, and that was it. We'd won the Derby and we'd done everything, not knowing, of course, that we had an unraced two-year-old who would change things."

That horse would eventually give Chenery, Turcotte, and Laurin the chance at an unprecedented second straight win together in the Kentucky Derby. When Secretariat finally arrived in Louisville, just thirteen days before the May 5 Derby, Sweat put him in the same stall given to Riva Ridge just a year earlier. Riva Ridge, however, had come into town on the crest of a career effort. Secretariat, by contrast, was only hours removed from the worst race of his life.

At face value his defeat in the Wood was baffling, and it could not have come at a more critical point. No longer was Secretariat untouchable. He had been knocked from his pedestal, and the fallout had led to concerns surrounding both his ability and his overall health. It triggered old fears that perhaps he was just another son of Bold Ruler who couldn't go the distance. There was extensive gossip, too. Some people

claimed that Secretariat was sore and run-down. Others said that he was training poorly, that his knees were bothering him, that by race day, he would be scratched. As usual, Secretariat — for better or worse — was the most talked-about horse on the grounds. Much of it was hot air.

"I'd seen that horse every morning for three months. There'd never been a bucket of ice near him, morning or afternoon," said Nack. "And now I'm reading Jimmy 'The Greek' Snyder in the Louisville *Courier-Journal* saying that this horse has got ice on his knees? Unbelievable."

"The scene in Louisville before the race was truly bizarre," Chenery recalled. "I don't think anything would prepare you for that fishbowl. The media attention was just excruciating. The rumors of his unsoundness were rampant. This just followed him through the week. Everybody was sure that something was going to be wrong with him."

The lip abscess continued to afflict Secretariat as the Derby drew near, and during his first serious exercise at Churchill Downs, a six-furlong drill in 1:12 3/5, he exhibited the same resentful attitude that he had shown at Aqueduct. Turcotte was flatly disappointed. Five days later, though, the jockey was convinced the Wood was an aberration. By then the abscess had suppurated, relieving the discomfort in Secretariat's mouth. When Turcotte climbed aboard for the colt's final tune-up on May 2, the change was obvious. Secretariat flew through five-eighths of a mile in :58 3/5, dazzling onlookers with his energy. He was tiptop once again.

Nevertheless, the backstretch buzz lingered like a dark cloud. The Wood was impossible to forget. Only a colossal comeback in the Derby would silence Secretariat's doubters and satisfy his investors. Past successes and championships were tossed aside. Secretariat's imminent future as a racehorse hinged on this mission.

"He had to win," Nack said. "If he did not win, there would be tremendous pressure from the syndicate to retire him immediately. It was absolutely crucial."

It would not be easy. Besides Angle Light the cast featured several divisional standouts, including Blue Grass winner My Gallant, Florida Derby champ Royal and Regal, and the road-tested Our Native, who had taken the Flamingo Stakes in early spring. The big gelding Forego had capped his preparation in splendid style, working five furlongs in :57 flat. Sham, in a fine move of his own, had knocked off three-quarters of a mile in a heady 1:11 1/5. His regular jockey, Laffit Pincay, had not ridden him in the Wood but would be reunited with the colt for the Derby. Despite the strength of the competition, Pincay was certain that Sham was primed for a king-sized performance. Only one rival, he felt, stood in Sham's way.

"I went into the race thinking the horse to beat was Secretariat," Pincay said. "I wasn't afraid of anybody else."

For all of Sham's potential, however, he did have a flaw, and it was magnified before the Derby began. As the thirteen-horse field filled the gate, the din from the crowd became too much for longshot Twice a Prince to handle. He suffered a meltdown, flipping over in his stall and delaying the break for several minutes. Sham, typically a poor starter, became unnerved, and he inadvertently banged his mouth against the gate doors. The incident dislodged two of his teeth, causing severe bleeding. Rattled, Sham was still among the vanguard that led the race into the first turn, and after a half-mile he began to pull into second place behind the sprinter Shecky Greene. Aside from a shaky beginning, things were setting up exactly the way Pincay had envisioned.

Pincay believed that Shecky Greene's furlongs were numbered — "I didn't think he would go the mile and one quarter," he said — and as Sham galloped along the backstretch, the rider was confident he had the pacesetter measured. Sham rapidly moved in as the final turn began, challenging Shecky Greene for the lead. The pair raced cheek by jowl around the bend, though Shecky Greene was straining just to hold his position. Before they had left the turn, Sham had put him away, and Pincay sensed nothing but power as the long Churchill Downs stretch approached. Just a quarter of a mile from the finish, before a multitude nearly 135,000 strong, Pincay felt he had the Kentucky Derby sewn up.

He did not know that Secretariat was closing in.

Unfazed by Twice a Prince's tantrum at the start, Secretariat had left

KINETIC/CHURCHILL DOWNS

**Penny Chenery, with her sister Margaret Carmichael and trainer Lucien Laurin**

the gate without fuss. Rather than hustle into the thick of the pace, Turcotte had instead stayed quiet, allowing the colt time to get his bearings. His game plan was simple: Let Secretariat ease through the first quarter-mile, then begin to make headway. Beneath The Meadow's familiar blue-and-white blocked silks, his face hooded in matching blinkers, Secretariat wasn't hard to spot early on. Less than a furlong into the Derby, he was in last place. Turcotte was not concerned.

"He was a horse that could be placed anywhere," explained the Hall of Fame jockey. "I wasn't sure conditioning-wise how much he benefited from the Wood Memorial. My idea of riding him in the Derby, if I was sure how much he got out of the Wood, was to put him into the running early. But as it turned out, I thought I would take it easy the first part and just pick it up from there on."

Secretariat ran as if he knew the strategy himself. Into the first turn he started to build steam, steadily passing rivals without a single cue from Turcotte. It was Turcotte's goal to avoid potential trouble, so he wisely kept Secretariat in the clear, racing in an outside path. After a deliberate :25 1/5 quarter-mile to begin with, the chestnut tossed in a second quarter on the curve in :24 flat. Up ahead Shecky Greene had broken free from the pack, completing his opening half in :47 2/5. This left Secretariat and Turcotte about ten lengths off the pace as they rolled onto the backstretch. They were now in sixth place, however, and Secretariat's speed continued to mount. His third quarter, elapsing in :23 4/5, carried him to fifth. When Sham finally engaged Shecky Greene three furlongs out, Secretariat, under the idle Turcotte, was sweeping into the picture behind them. Compared to the horse who had seemed so lackluster at Aqueduct, Secretariat was moving with purpose.

"To see him go down the backside," Nack remembered, "doing things that he had not done two weeks before in the Wood — picking up horses, moving with that same powerful stride — and to see him all of a sudden in contention, right there, he looked like his old self. When he turned for home, his coat was radiant. He looked like he was on fire."

Powering around the far turn, he whipped past longshots Gold Bag and Royal and Regal, then blew by Shecky Greene, completing a :23 2/5 quarter-mile, his fastest thus far. Ahead, only Sham remained. Turcotte could see that Sham was moving fluidly, that Pincay was still sitting motionless. Fittingly, the Kentucky Derby would now be decided by the race's two principal contenders. The battle many had expected to see in the Wood Memorial — Secretariat and Sham trading blows down to the wire — was about to play out before a record Churchill Downs audience.

Instead, it was over by midstretch. Sham aimed for home holding a one-length lead, and Pincay had not yet turned him loose. For several strides the jockey was convinced he was about to win his first Kentucky Derby. Shecky Greene was gone, and there was no other threat in sight. Pincay heard nobody coming from behind. A split-second later, Secretariat burst into view to his right, and to Pincay's shock, he was pulling away from Sham.

"He went by me like nothing. I couldn't believe it," he remembered. "I had so much horse, and when I started hand-riding Sham, he just gave it to me. It felt like he accelerated. He was reaching out, and usually when you feel that way, you just never get beat. I was surprised that he could go by me so easy."

Even more astonishing was Secretariat's finish. He dispatched Sham for good near the eighth pole, steadily extending his advantage from there. Turcotte did not push him through the final furlong — the race was already well in hand — yet Secretariat still crossed the line in 1:59 2/5. His stretch run, starting at the quarter pole, had taken just :23 flat. Never before had a Derby winner closed with such speed. Moreover, Secretariat had covered the distance in remarkable fashion: Each of his quarter-miles had been faster than the one before it.

There was further magnitude in his triumph. Secretariat had effaced Northern Dancer's track record for ten furlongs. He had overwhelmed his competition, carrying Turcotte from last to first with a move rarely seen from a Thoroughbred, experienced or otherwise. He had provided a posthumous milestone for Bold Ruler, who had died when Secretariat was just a yearling. He had wiped out the memory of the Wood and disproved all the rumors that had surfaced in its aftermath. All of this had taken less than two minutes.

Lost in the whirl of Secretariat's victory was the excellent effort of Sham. Although Sham could not match Secretariat as they drove toward the wire, none of the others came close to catching him for second place. Our Native eventually edged Forego for third, but Sham was far ahead of them. He had come through with the race of his life, finishing two and a half lengths behind Secretariat. Thus Sham, despite his defeat, had done what no other horse had previously accomplished: Like Secretariat, he had broken the two-minute mark in the Derby.

The tone had been set, for when they squared off two weeks later in the Preakness Stakes at Pimlico, the results were the same. Taking control much sooner than he had in the Derby, Secretariat again defeated Sham by two and a half lengths. By that point the enthusiasm

## Kentucky Derby
## Purse: $125,000 Added

**9th Race Churchill Downs - May 5, 1973. Ninety-ninth running Kentucky Derby.**
**Purse $125,000 added. Three-year-olds. 1 1-4 Miles. Main Track. Track: Fast.**
**Value of race $198,800. Net value to winner, $155,050 and gold trophy; second, $25,000; third, $12,500; fourth, $6,250.**

| Horse | A | Wgt | Eqp | Odds | PP | 1/4 | 1/2 | 3/4 | 1 | Str | Fin | Jockey |
|---|---|---|---|---|---|---|---|---|---|---|---|---|
| Secretariat | 3 | 126 | b | a-1.50 | 10 | $11^{h}$ | $6^{1/2}$ | $5^{1}$ | $2^{1 1/2}$ | $1^{1/2}$ | $1^{2 1/2}$ | R Turcottte |
| Sham | 3 | 126 | b | 2.50 | 4 | $5^{1}$ | $3^{2}$ | $2^{1}$ | $1^{1/2}$ | $2^{6}$ | $2^{8}$ | L Pincay Jr |
| Our Native | 3 | 126 | b | 10.60 | 7 | $6^{1/2}$ | $8^{1 1/2}$ | $8^{1}$ | $5^{h}$ | $3^{h}$ | $3^{1/2}$ | D Brumfield |
| Forego | 3 | 126 | | 28.60 | 9 | $9^{1 1/2}$ | $9^{1/2}$ | $6^{1/2}$ | $6^{2}$ | $4^{1/2}$ | $4^{2 1/2}$ | P Anderson |
| Restless Jet | 3 | 126 | | 28.50 | 1 | $7^{1 1/2}$ | $7^{h}$ | $10^{1 1/2}$ | $7^{1 1/2}$ | $6^{1 1/2}$ | $5^{2 1/2}$ | M Hole |
| Shecky Greene | 3 | 126 | b | b-5.70 | 11 | $1^{1 1/2}$ | $1^{3}$ | $1^{1 1/2}$ | $3^{3}$ | $5^{1}$ | $6^{1 1/2}$ | L Adams |
| Navajo | 3 | 126 | b | 52.30 | 5 | $10^{1 1/2}$ | $10^{1}$ | $11^{4}$ | $8^{1 1/2}$ | $8^{2}$ | $7^{no}$ | W Soirez |
| Royal and Regal | 3 | 126 | | 28.30 | 8 | $3^{1}$ | $4^{3}$ | $4^{3}$ | $4^{1}$ | $7^{1 1/2}$ | $8^{3 1/2}$ | W Blum |
| My Gallant | 3 | 126 | b | b-5.70 | 12 | $8^{h}$ | $11^{1 1/2}$ | $12^{3}$ | $11^{2}$ | $10^{1/2}$ | $9^{h}$ | B Baeza |
| Angle Light | 3 | 126 | | a-1.50 | 2 | $4^{h}$ | $5^{1 1/2}$ | $7^{1}$ | $10^{1 1/2}$ | $9^{1 1/2}$ | $10^{1 1/2}$ | J LeBlanc |
| Gold Bag | 3 | 126 | b | 68.30 | 13 | $2^{h}$ | $2^{h}$ | $3^{1/2}$ | $9^{1}$ | $11^{1}$ | $11^{no}$ | E Fires |
| Twice a Prince | 3 | 126 | b | 62.50 | 6 | 13 | 13 | 13 | 13 | $12^{2}$ | $12^{1 1/2}$ | A Santiago |
| Warbucks | 3 | 126 | | 7.20 | 3 | $12^{1}$ | $12^{3}$ | $9^{h}$ | $12^{1 1/2}$ | 13 | 13 | W Hartack |

a-Coupled Secretariat and Angle Light; b-Shecky Greene and My Gallant.

**Off Time:** 5:37 **Time Of Race:** :23⅖ :47⅖ 1:11⅘ 1:36⅕ 1:59⅖ (new track record)
**Start:** Good For All **Track:** Fast
**Equipment:** b for blinkers

**Mutuel Payoffs**

| | | | | |
|---|---|---|---|---|
| 1A | Secretariat | $5.00 | $3.20 | $3.00 |
| 5 | Sham | | 3.20 | 3.00 |
| 8 | Our Native | | | 4.20 |

**Winner:** Secretariat, ch. c. by Bold Ruler—Somethingroyal, by Princequillo (Trained by L. Laurin). Bred by Meadow Stud Inc. in Va.

**Start good. Won handily.**
SECRETARIAT relaxed nicely and dropped back last leaving the gate as the field broke in good order, moved between horses to begin improving position entering the first turn, but passed rivals from the outside thereafter. Turcotte roused him smartly with the whip in his right hand leaving the far turn and SECRETARIAT strongly raced to the leaders, lost a little momentum racing into the stretch where Turcotte used the whip again, but then switched it to his left hand and merely flashed it as the winner willingly drew away in record-breaking time. SHAM, snugly reserved within striking distance after brushing with NAVAJO at the start, raced around rivals to the front without any need of rousing and drew clear between calls entering the stretch, was under a strong hand ride after being displaced in the last furlong and continued resolutely to dominate the remainder of the field. OUR NATIVE, reserved in the first run through the stretch, dropped back slightly on the turn, came wide in the drive and finished well for his placing. FOREGO, taken to the inside early, veered slightly from a rival and hit the rail entering the far turn, swung wide entering the stretch and vied with OUR NATIVE in the drive. RESTLESS JET saved ground in an even effort. SHECKY GREENE easily set the pace under light rating for nearly seven furlongs and faltered. NAVAJO was outrun. ROYAL AND REGAL raced well for a mile and had nothing left in the drive. MY GALLANT, outrun at all stages, was crowded on the stretch turn. ANGLE LIGHT gave way steadily in a dull effort and was forced to check when crowded by GOLD BAG on the stretch turn. GOLD BAG had good speed and stopped. TWICE A PRINCE reared and was hung in the gate briefly before the start and then showed nothing in the running. WARBUCKS was dull.

**Owners:** (1) Meadow Stable; (2) S Sommer; (3) Pritchard, Thomas, & Resseguet; (4) Lazy F Ranch; (5) Elkwood Farm; (6) J Kellman; (7) J Stevenson-R Stump; (8) Aisco Stable; (9) A I Appleton; (10) E Whittaker; (11) R Sechrest-Gottdank; (12) Elmendorf; (13) E E Elzemeyer


surrounding Secretariat's chase for Thoroughbred racing's first Triple Crown since Citation's in 1948 was sweeping across the country. In the wake of the Preakness, Secretariat became an instant icon, and his transcendent popularity even saw him grace the covers of *Time*, *Newsweek*, and *Sports Illustrated*.

Excitement for his attempt at history in the June 9 Belmont Stakes reached a fever pitch. Secretariat responded with a display that still

stands as the most unforgettable in modern Thoroughbred racing. He clinched the sport's ninth Triple Crown with an incredible thirty-one length triumph, and in the process, he established a world record of 2:24 for a mile and a half on dirt. Neither his margin of victory nor his stakes mark has been eclipsed since.

For Sham, however, the Belmont marked the end of the line. Although he had carried himself courageously in both the Derby and Preakness, the two losses took a definite toll. Before the Belmont he appeared gaunt, and he ran at only a fraction of his ability. A half-mile in, Sham began to back out of contention, unable to keep pace with Secretariat, and he ultimately finished a badly beaten last. He never raced again.

The two have been entwined in history ever since, and their classic encounter in the Kentucky Derby forms much of the fabric that makes the 1973 Triple Crown so enduring. In any other year Sham's run in the Derby would have resulted in victory, yet he is remembered solely as a worthy but conquered opponent. It is Secretariat whose exploits continue to charm newcomers and astound hardboots. Each May another gate full of three-year-olds comes and goes, and with every Derby that passes, the aura of that memorable afternoon is further enhanced. There is a magic to it now, and those privileged to witness it firsthand know that they had brushed up against a legend. For some, that's enough to soften the blow of defeat.

"There are so many races where you come back and say, 'Maybe I should have done this or maybe I should have done that, then maybe it would have been a different outcome.' You second-guess what you did in the race," Pincay explained. "But with a horse like that, there's nothing you can do. Actually, I think Secretariat was the best horse I've ever seen. The things he did nobody has done, so you don't feel so bad about it. You're just happy you finished second. He was just unbelievable."

*By Craig Harzmann*

# Viva Canonero!
## (Canonero II, 1971)

THERE IS A CHAPTER in the annals of Thoroughbred racing and the Kentucky Derby that sadly has withered with the years. But beyond the faded words and photos, beyond the madness that swept through the sport in the spring of 1971, the legend of Canonero II cries out to be told after all these years.

No detailed introduction is needed, for nothing can prepare the reader for the incredible tale about to unfold. The opening chapter begins in the rolling hills of Kentucky, where most sagas of the Turf unfold, and ends in the barn of Venezuelan trainer Juan Arias. From this unlikely place emerged a skinny, crooked-legged colt who would arrive at Churchill Downs for the ninety-seventh Kentucky Derby a forlorn-looking creature, ridiculed by the entire racing community. By the time he departed, however, he no longer was a clown, but a hero known throughout the Western Hemisphere as "The Caracas Cannonball."

At the 1967 Keeneland fall breeding stock sale, horsemen gathered as they do every year in search of bargain-basement bloodstock. Among the numerous broodmares sold that year was the six-year-old Nantallah mare, Dixieland II, in foal to the young stallion Pretendre, runner-up in the previous year's English Derby at Epsom Downs. The pedigree held little interest to American breeders, and when the bidding stopped at $2,700, Claiborne Farm manager William Taylor, acting as agent for Dixieland II's breeder, Edward B. Benjamin, took it upon himself to buy the mare back. Benjamin then gave the mare to Taylor, who told him he could have her back any time he wanted.

Several months later, just before Dixieland II foaled, Benjamin told Taylor he had changed his mind and wanted her back.

Dixieland II gave birth to her Pretendre colt on April 24, 1968, at Claiborne Farm, where Benjamin boarded his horses. Benjamin tried to sell the colt the following year at the Keeneland July yearling sale, but the horse was rejected due to his crooked right foreleg. He was so awkward and ungainly someone commented that he "had a stride like a crab." Benjamin consigned him to the then less-prestigious September yearling sale, where one could sell just about anything. But even at this sale a deformed colt by an unfashionable European stallion, out of a mare that couldn't even bring more than $2,700, had little hope of selling, especially on the last day of the sale. That is unless someone was willing to pick him up for practically nothing.

Venezuelan bloodstock agent Luis Navas, who had a reputation as an equine junk dealer, was that someone. Navas would buy young horses at dirt-cheap prices, then put together package deals and sell them to Venezuelan owners who were willing to pay decent prices for American-bred youngsters. Navas, acting under the name Albert, agent, made one bid of $1,200 and the colt was his. He immediately packaged him up with a Ballymoss colt and a filly and sold them to Venezuelan businessman Pedro Baptista for $60,000.

Baptista was forty-four years old, but his bald head, scar on his nose, and missing teeth made him look older. This wasn't a particularly good time for Baptista to be buying horses. His plumbing and pipe manufacturing company was in dire financial straits, and he was on the verge of bankruptcy. To continue purchasing horses, he registered them under the name of his son-in-law, Edgar Caibett. After Navas sent him his three new yearlings, Baptista turned them over to a young, up-and-coming trainer named Juan Arias.

Arias was born in 1938 in the small town of Marin in Yaracuy State. His family moved to the slums of Caracas, where his father abandoned him. Raised by his mother and grandmother, he escaped into the world of horses, whose beauty provided a stark contrast to the poverty in which he lived. Whenever he could, he would sneak away to the racetrack, where he would clean out stalls for free. When he turned sixteen, he enrolled in trainer's school at the old El Paraiso Racetrack, after which he got his first full-time job at the track. With little pay and nowhere to live, he slept in the stalls. He eventually began to put a small string together and several years later was introduced to Baptista, who took a liking to him and gave him sixteen horses to train.

One of the horses arriving at Arias' barn in the spring of 1970 was that ungainly colt from the Keeneland sale, whom Baptista had named Canonero after a type of singing group. Baptista had been forced to sell twenty-four of his forty-eight horses to raise some cash, and his instructions to Arias were to get started quickly and have the colt ready to win first time out. When Arias first laid eyes on Canonero, the trainer knew he had his work cut out for him. Not only was the colt's crooked leg still noticeable, but Canonero had a split right hoof and a bad case of worms. Arias had to clean out the colt's stomach every thirty days and put him on a special diet, which included seaweed from Australia.

Although Canonero had numerous physical problems, he showed promise in the morning and didn't need much training to get in shape. He made his debut at La Rinconada (which opened after El Paraiso closed down) on August 8, 1970, and despite being sent off at 12-1 in the six-furlong race, he won by six and a half lengths. Baptista, who was considered an eccentric, then came up with a plan to send him to the United States to race at Del Mar in the hopes of getting him sold.

In his first start, an allowance event, the repatriated colt raced under the name Canonero II, because a horse with the name Canonero had already been racing in the United States. After finishing third at 21-1 in the allowance, Canonero finished fifth in the Del Mar Futurity, beaten seven and three-quarters lengths in 1:08 4/5. One trainer at Del Mar, Charlie Whittingham, thought the colt had promise, and when he heard Canonero could be purchased for about $70,000, he attempted to buy him for one of his main clients, Mary Jones. Unfortunately, no one with the horse could speak English. Unable to get a firm price, Whittingham gave up, and Canonero returned to Venezuela.

Having failed to sell the horse, Baptista told Arias, "Don't worry, we'll win the Kentucky Derby next year."

Arias replied, "The Kentucky Derby? What's that?"

Canonero won his next two races; then, following two defeats, he stretched out to a mile and a quarter on March 7, 1971, and defeated older horses in 2:03 2/5, with new rider Gustavo Avila aboard. Here it was only March, and Canonero had already beaten older horses and won at the Derby distance, two feats unheard of in the United States. A week later he dropped back to a sprint and finished third before winning his next two starts. On April 10 he stretched back out to nine furlongs and finished third, carrying 112 pounds. It was his ninth start in four months and his fifth in the last thirty-five days.

Baptista then hurled a bombshell at Arias, telling him he seriously wanted to run Canonero in the Kentucky Derby, which was only three weeks away. Little did Baptista realize, however, how close the horse had come to not being nominated. That February, Baptista was in Florida and heard that Pimlico vice president Chick Lang was there taking nominations for the Preakness and might do him a favor and put in the nominations for the Derby and Belmont as well. Baptista found out that Lang was staying at the Miami Springs Villas near Hialeah and called him.

Also staying at the hotel were John Finney and Larry Ensor from the Fasig-Tipton Sales Company. "I get this call from a guy with a Spanish accent who says his name is Baptista," Lang recalled. "I immediately thought it was a joke because the guys from Fasig-Tipton and I were always playing practical jokes on each other. When he said his name was Baptista, I kept thinking of the guy that Castro had removed from power in Cuba and thought someone was pulling my leg.

"He said he had a horse he wanted to nominate for the Preakness named Canonero. I said, 'Who are you?' and he told me he was the owner. I told him to spell the horse's name because I had never heard of him. He said, 'You will.' "

Lang wrote the nomination down on the back of a cocktail napkin and told Baptista he'd contact the representatives for the Derby and

THE BLOOD-HORSE

**A pre-Derby canter around the Churchill Downs oval**

Belmont and put in those nominations as well. After Lang hung up, he went in the other room where Finney and Ensor were having evening cocktails. Finney asked who was on the phone, and Lang said, "I don't know; I thought it was you playing a joke on me." Finney assured Lang it wasn't he. Lang then asked him if he'd ever heard of a horse named Canonero. Finney left the room and did some checking, then came back a few minutes later and said, "Someone's pulling your leg; I can't find any horse by that name."

Lang took the napkin out of his pocket and started to crumple it up and throw it in the trash, but he decided he'd better put in the nomination and if it turned out to phony, so be it. The following day he phoned in the nomination to the racing secretary's office but had them check first to see if the horse really existed. They processed the nomination and found that the horse was legitimate.

With the Derby getting close, Baptista, according to his close friend and adviser, Miguel Torrealba, had a dream in which his deceased mother told him Canonero was going to win the Kentucky Derby. That was good enough for him.

Meanwhile, in the United States the Derby picture was wide-open following injuries to early favorites Hoist the Flag and His Majesty and the defection of Flamingo winner Executioner, who would wait for the Preakness. The big horses remaining were the indefatigable Jim French, the Santa Anita Derby winner who had already run in nine stakes across the country that year; San Felipe Handicap and California Derby winner Unconscious; the Calumet Farm entry of Bold and Able and Florida Derby winner Eastern Fleet; and Blue Grass Stakes winner Impetuosity.

One week after his third-place finish at La Rinconada, Canonero boarded a plane for Miami with his groom, Juan Quintero, whose expenses came out Arias' pocket. The colt was sent without any papers or blood work. Shortly after taking off, the plane was forced to return due to mechanical failure. The second attempt wasn't any more successful as one of the engines caught on fire and the plane had to return once again. The only other plane they could find was a cargo plane filled with chickens and ducks, which became Canonero's travel companions.

Finally, a weary Canonero arrived in Miami. But airport officials quickly discovered the horse had no papers, so he was forced to remain on the plane for twelve hours in the sweltering heat, nearly becoming dehydrated. With the papers finally in order, Canonero was allowed off the plane. One report, from someone close to Baptista, said the colt actually was forced to fly to Panama and wait there until the papers were in order. In any event, Canonero was back in the United States, but with no blood test results, officials placed him in quarantine for four days while his blood work was sent to a U.S. Department of Agriculture lab in Beltsville, Maryland.

By the time he was released from quarantine, Canonero had lost about seventy pounds and was a physical mess. But his problems were far from over. Baptista had not sent enough money to pay for a flight from Miami to Louisville, so Canonero had to be vanned the 1,200 miles, a trip that took nearly twenty-four hours. Neither Arias nor Quintero could speak English, and when the van arrived at the Churchill Downs stable gate, no one at the track had any idea who the horse or the trainer was. After a short while, the matter was resolved, and Canonero was allowed entrance into Churchill Downs. The Kentucky Derby, set for May 1, was one week away.

When Canonero's name popped unexpectedly into the Derby picture, the Caliente Future Book quoted him at odds of 500-1.

Canonero's stay at Churchill became a freak show, as curiosity seekers would come by just to take a look at this harlequin of a horse. Instead of a conventional forelock, he sported bangs, much like Moe of the Three Stooges, and every one of his ribs could be counted. When Arias inquired how much a sack of bran cost, he was told forty-five dollars. "Too much," he said. "Can we have half a sack?"

Arias became almost as much of a curiosity as his horse. Here was a black man from Venezuela who spoke no English, who was rarely seen without a cigarette in his mouth, and who usually wore a sport jacket and tie to the barn in the morning.

All the while, Arias kept what little media that showed up at the barn amused by telling them that Canonero was a horse of destiny and would win the Kentucky Derby. He trained Canonero whenever the horse felt like training, and the times he did, Arias put up a 165-pound exercise rider and had him gallop the colt without a saddle. When reporters asked Arias what Canonero was going to do on a particular day, the trainer would go through a pantomime of a horse galloping. Louisville horseman Jose Rodriguez, a native of Puerto Rico, was helping out Arias, serving as his assistant and interpreter.

Canonero and Arias had almost a spiritual relationship. If the horse didn't eat, Arias would go into his stall and talk to him and pet him, and he would start eating. If he felt Canonero had something to say to him, he'd press his ear against the horse and listen. Before sending him out to the track, he'd ask Canonero how he was feeling and how he slept the night before. If Canonero "told" him he didn't feel like training that day, Arias would say, "Okay, if you don't feel like it, I won't force you. Just relax, go eat, and wait for tomorrow."

Quintero took almost the same kind of approach. "I speak to him with affection and love," he said. "In other words, I treat him like I was raising my own son."

The "Canonero Show" became a running joke, especially when he finally did work, crawling a half-mile in a lethargic :53 4/5. But what was lost behind all the laughter was that Canonero was beginning to thrive physically and had put back fifty of the seventy pounds he had lost.

Through an interpreter Arias tried to explain to people that he knew his horse, but few listened. "I have my methods," he said. "Most of the American trainers train for speed. I train Canonero to be a star, a horse of depth who is versatile and can be ridden in front or from behind. They say I work my horse too slow. Let's see if he runs that slow on Saturday."

Three days before the Derby, jockey Gustavo Avila arrived at Churchill Downs. Known in Venezuela as "El Monstruo," or "The Monster," Avila was one of the country's leading jockeys and had ridden Canonero on three occasions earlier in the year, winning twice.

So little was known about Canonero and his record in Venezuela, the *Daily Racing Form* past performance lines for his last three starts did not provide the name or conditions of the race, the jockey, weight, first three finishers, and comments. All it said was, "Missing data unavailable at this time."

Arias was invited to a pre-Derby party and felt as if some people there were mocking Canonero. "They made us very mad," he recalled. "They made fun of our horse. They said his workout was no good. They said we're clowns and we're crazy. They came to see my horse and turned away and wrinkled up their noses. Someone wrote he crawls like a turtle."

Arias said one rival owner proposed a mock toast, holding up his glass of champagne to him and saying, "Mucha suerte" (good luck in Spanish).

On Derby morning Arias worked Canonero under the cover of darkness. This time he put a saddle on him to let the colt know it was time to get serious. Canonero was razor-sharp, breezing three furlongs in about :35, a workout that was not revealed until two years later.

Unconscious was made the 5-2 favorite, with the Calumet entry 7-2, and Jim French 9-2. Canonero was put in the six-horse mutuel field, which closed at a meager 8-1. Baptista decided not to attend the Derby, and instead stayed home to take care of business, while sending his son to represent him. Avila put on Baptista's brown silks and brown cap and headed out to get his instructions from Arias.

Arias accompanied Canonero to the paddock but was too nervous to saddle the colt and left that task to Jose Rodriguez. Instead of going up to the boxes, Arias watched the race from the rail, along with the grooms.

As the field of twenty broke from the gate, Canonero immediately dropped to the back of the pack. When they charged past Arias, the colt was sixteenth, already some twenty lengths off the lead. The pace was a strong one, with Bold and Able, the lesser of the Calumet Farm entry, battling with three mutuel field horses — Barbizon Streak, Jr's Arrowhead, and Knight Counter.

By the time the field hit the backstretch, after a quarter in :23 and a half in :46 4/5, Canonero had dropped back to eighteenth and was still about twenty lengths off the pace. Bold and Able shook off the three longshots and opened a two-length lead as the horses headed down the backstretch. His stablemate, Eastern Fleet, began to move closer along the inside as the field bunched up a bit. Avila steered Canonero to the outside to give him a clear run, but he was still back near the rear of the pack.

Bold and Able, still leading by a length and a half, hit the far turn in a solid 1:11 3/5 for the six furlongs. Eastern Fleet moved strongly into second, with the favorite, Unconscious, a couple of lengths back in fifth. Jim French, who had been in mid-pack throughout, maintained his position and was about to launch his bid. Canonero had inched closer but still was in fifteenth, with eighteen lengths to make up and only a half-mile in which to do it.

Around the far turn Eastern Fleet charged up inside Bold and Able, and the two Calumet colts battled head and head, while opening a clear lead on their closest pursuers. It looked like a flashback to the Calumet glory days when the famed devil's red-and-blue silks dominated Thoroughbred racing. Unconscious and Jim French were getting in gear, but then all eyes caught sight of a brown blur streaking past horses

as if it were moving in a faster time frame than the others.

"Who is that?" everyone in attendance and watching on television asked. Even as the mysterious figure came hurtling out of the turn and engulfed the two Calumet colts, no one had a clue who it was except Arias and his Venezuelan entourage, who already were jumping up and down and screaming "Canonero! Canonero!"

Canonero charged by the Calumet duo as if they had run into a brick wall. With Avila just hand-riding him, he quickly drew clear, while still racing on his left lead. He opened a three-length lead at the eighth pole and continued to pour it on. Jim French finally found his

THE BLOOD-HORSE

**As Canonero hits the wire well in the clear, those watching ask, "Who is that?"**

best stride and clear sailing and came with a strong late run, but Canonero was long gone. He crossed the wire three and three-quarters lengths in front, still on his wrong lead. As soon as he crossed the finish line, most everyone simultaneously scrolled down the names of the horses in their program to see who had won the Kentucky Derby. Even after they had matched up the number fifteen horse with the name, many still had no idea who it was.

Up in the press box even the majority of reporters didn't know who had won. When Chick Lang heard who it was, the name didn't ring a bell. After the horses had pulled up and the winner came jogging back, it finally hit him "like a bolt of lightning."

The horse whose name he had scribbled down on the back of a cocktail napkin and almost tossed in the garbage had just won the Kentucky Derby. "Jesus Christ!" he shouted. "It's the mystery horse. I can't believe it. This is like a fairy tale."

Reporters in the press box could not believe it either. It was the horse they had been mocking for the past week. Quasimodo had turned into Prince Charming right before their eyes.

Arias burst into tears and dashed onto the track where he hugged Quintero and just about everyone else who spoke Spanish. But the indignities were not over. When he tried to go into the winner's circle, the security guards wouldn't let him in. It was a repeat of the scene that had played out at the stable gate entrance a week earlier. Fortunately, one of his fellow countrymen who spoke English explained who Arias was and the Derby-winning trainer was allowed in.

Meanwhile, back in Caracas, Pedro Baptista had no idea what had happened. When a friend called ten minutes after the race and shouted into the phone that Baptista had just won the Kentucky Derby, the owner thought it was a joke and hung up. But the friend called back and swore he was telling the truth. Then, when the phone began ringing non-stop, Baptista, like Arias, broke into tears. He told his father the news and the two of them had a good cry. They then drove to the cemetery, where they prayed over the grave of Baptista's mother, who had paid him that fateful visit in his dreams.

That night Baptista threw a party for some two hundred guests. After twenty hours of revelry and drinking vino punche — a mixture of lemon, bitters, and "mucho" whiskey — Baptista told his guests the party would continue until Tuesday when Avila returned.

By then Caracas was in full celebration, with people singing and dancing throughout the city. When Avila returned, he was carried through the streets of Caracas. He also received a telegram from the president of Venezuela, which read in part: "This great victory will stimulate Venezuela's progress in all its efforts ..."

For Arias there wasn't much time for celebration. He and Quintero had to pack up and head to Baltimore for the Preakness. They had won the Derby, and now it was time to start thinking about a sweep of the Triple Crown, a feat that hadn't been accomplished in twenty-three years.

Arias said the one thing that gave him satisfaction following the Derby was running into the owner who had given him the mock toast before the race. When Arias saw him, the trainer raised his hand as if proposing a toast, and said, "Mucha suerte."

Perhaps the headline that best described the Derby appeared in *Sports Illustrated*. It read: "Missing Data Unavailable," referring not only to the comment in the *Daily Racing Form* past performances, but also to the mystery and confusion surrounding this curious invader from South America.

When Arias and Canonero arrived at Pimlico, more problems awaited them. Shortly after arriving, Canonero refused to eat. All communication between Arias and veterinarian Ralph Yergey was conducted through an interpreter, and it was debatable whether he actually was interpreting anything Arias and Yergey were saying. Canonero was developing a case of thrush, a foot infection usually caused by a horse standing in his own urine, an ordeal that Canonero was subjected to while in quarantine. The morning after the Derby, Chick Lang went to visit the colt and observed the same conditions.

Not only did Canonero have foot problems, but he also was cutting his tongue on a loose baby tooth, and he had contracted a low-grade fever. Six days before the race his medication was switched from pen-strep, a standard antibiotic mixture, to ampicillin because the lidocaine in the pen-strep would have showed up in the urine.

Despite Canonero's victory in the Derby, very few people were convinced the race wasn't a fluke. The final time was a slow 2:03 1/5, and Canonero's running style of coming from twenty lengths back was not suitable to the Preakness, which was run at a shorter distance and over a speed-favoring track with tighter turns. Eastern Fleet looked to be the perfect Preakness-type horse, and many of the "experts" seemed to favor him over Canonero.

Disdain for the Derby winner grew after Canonero worked a snail-like five furlongs in 1:06. One trainer commented afterward, "That was about a fifth of a second faster than might have been expected of a plow horse." Another said, "If I had that horse and he worked that slow, I'd put him on the first slow boat to South America."

Arias, however, was thrilled with the work. "Perfecto!" he said. "He's ready for Saturday." He later told the Baltimore *Sun*, "They laughed at us in Louisville, and they are laughing at us in Baltimore. But it is we who will be laughing at the whole racing world!"

What people didn't realize was that there was more to Canonero than what appeared on the surface. When a Baltimore radiologist, Dr. George Burke, took an electrocardiogram of the horse, he discovered the animal's heartbeat was only thirty beats per minute, which was five fewer than the average horse. "Fantastic; that's about as low as a horse will go," Burke said. A low heartbeat signifies exceptional stamina.

Canonero and Jim French were made co-favorites at 3-1, with Eastern Fleet the main danger to steal the race, getting bet down to 6-1. This time Baptista came for the race. What happened next was in some ways even more remarkable than what was witnessed on the first Saturday in May. Eastern Fleet, as expected, shot to the lead, but to everyone's shock, here was Canonero bursting out of the gate from post position nine and taking up the chase.

Canonero collared the Calumet runner as they turned up the back-stretch, and the pair were at each other's throat every step of the way

down the backstretch and around the far turn. After a half in :47, they sizzled the next quarter in :23 2/5, while opening up five lengths on the rest of the field. The farther they went, the more they opened up.

With three-quarters run in a demanding 1:10 2/5, and the mile in 1:35, someone had to crack, and it was Eastern Fleet. Canonero, despite having run six furlongs four and two-fifth seconds (or twenty-two lengths) faster than he had in the Derby, showed no signs of tiring. He drew clear of Eastern Fleet inside the eighth pole and, again on his wrong lead, crossed the wire a length and a half in front, with Eastern Fleet four and a half lengths ahead of Jim French. The horse that people laughed at as being as slow as a "plow horse" had just run the mile and three-sixteenths in 1:54, breaking Nashua's track record by three-fifths of a second.

Back in Venezuela five million people watched the race on television, and again the country erupted in celebration. Baptista headed to the winner's circle pumping his fist, then pointing it up to the sky, shouting, "Belmont! Belmont! Belmont!"

**Canonero and his confident connections**

When asked how he felt, Baptista said, "We have come up here — two Indians (he and Avila) and a black man (Arias) with a horse that nobody believed in, and we're destroying two hundred years of American racing tradition, dominated by the cream of your society. This is a monumental event for international relations. You can't imagine the impact this has had in Venezuela. Canonero is truly a horse of the people."

Arias was asked how he got Canonero to run so fast off such a slow work. All he said in response was, "They could not hold back destiny."

Before vanning to Belmont for the final leg of his amazing journey, "The Caracas Cannonball," as Canonero was being hailed, was honored at Pimlico between the fourth and fifth races. He was led onto the track to the playing of the Venezuelan national anthem, with the applause building as he approached the finish line. In the winner's circle Maryland Governor Marvin Mandel signed a document proclaiming the six members of the Canonero team honorary citizens of Maryland.

When Canonero arrived at Belmont Park, a circus had replaced the freak show of Churchill Downs. Between veterinarians and advisers for Baptista all trying to run the show, Arias also had to deal with new physical problems that were plaguing Canonero, as well as some of the old ones. The colt still was suffering from thrush, and now his right hock was swollen. He had burned his heels while galloping at Belmont, and he came down with a severe skin disease that covered a good portion of his body.

Security was posted at his barn twenty-four hours a day. He even appeared on the *Today Show* when former Major League Baseball player and author Joe Garagiola came out to the barn to "interview" him. Canonero was brought out, and Garagiola stuck a microphone in his face and began asking him questions, such as "Where'd you get that haircut?"

Canonero's physical problems forced him to miss a couple of days of training. Like at Churchill and Pimlico, the jokes started up. There was no way a horse in this condition could win the Belmont. "They still think we're a bunch of crazy Indians," Arias said.

But deep down Arias knew Canonero would not be at his best. Veterinarian William O. Reed examined the Triple Crown hopeful and told Arias the colt was only 75 percent ready to go a mile and a half. Even *Sports Illustrated* tried to convince Arias and Baptista not to run. An editorial that appeared in the magazine a week before the Belmont read: "Perhaps sometime before the Belmont this Saturday, Canonero's handlers will forego false national pride and scratch the horse. We hope so. He is in bad shape and has been for a week."

Arias knew in his heart Canonero probably shouldn't run, but there was too much at stake, and the trainer still believed his horse could win the race. After all, this was a horse of destiny. All of Venezuela had gone mad over the colt, and throughout the country came the cries of "Viva Canonero!"

Plans were in the works to erect a statue of Canonero at La Rinconada. Songs about Canonero were being played on the radio. At one civil registry office in Venezuela, a couple submitted the name Canonero Segundo (Canonero the second) for their newborn son. At Belmont a film was being made called *The Ballad of Canonero*, featuring a song of the same name. It was later shown on television and was named best sports film of the year by the Fifteenth Annual International Film and TV Festival of New York. It was too late to turn back now.

A group of about two thousand Venezuelans made the trip for the Belmont, many wearing T-shirts reading, "Viva Canonero!" and "Viva Venezuela!" New York's Puerto Rican community adopted Canonero, and Puerto Ricans and other Hispanics poured into the track by the thousands. The official crowd was listed at 82,694, destroying the previous record of 67,961. The new mark would stand for twenty-eight years.

Hours before the race, radio broadcasters in Venezuela asked the people to honk their car horns and churches to peal their bells at the precise same moment. Right before the race the city of Caracas was like a ghost town, with its citizens glued to their televisions.

Canonero's many maladies proved much stronger than destiny. The colt went to the front and ran as far and as fast as his battle-weary legs and body could take him. He tried gallantly but could finish no better than fourth, beaten only four and a half lengths by longshot Pass Catcher. Even as the Derby/Preakness winner began to fade turning for home, cries of "Canonero" still resounded from the huge grandstand. Jim French and Bold Reason, two colts Canonero had already man-handled, finished second and third, respectively.

The morning after the race Dr. Reed examined Canonero and said the gallant warrior still was showing signs of extreme fatigue. Baptista looked at the defeat philosophically and told those close to the horse not to hold their heads down. "Be cheerful," he said. "We have become rich and famous, the horse is all right, and the future is ahead of us."

Baptista had turned down several lucrative offers for Canonero but felt the time was now right to sell. Shortly after the Belmont he sold Canonero to Robert Kleberg, owner of King Ranch, for $1.5 million.

Canonero did not run again until the following May, losing his first six races. It was obvious he no longer was the same horse. His best effort was a second in the Carter Handicap in his first race back.

His new trainer, William J. "Buddy" Hirsch, tried blinkers, but that didn't help. As a last resort he summoned Canonero's old jockey, Gustavo Avila, to come up from Venezuela to ride Canonero in a mile and one-sixteenth allowance race at Belmont. Canonero showed some of his old spark, dashing to the lead and setting sizzling fractions of :45 2/5 and 1:09 1/5 before tiring to finish fifth. With the sleeping giant now showing signs of awakening, Hirsch and Avila agreed that a return to blinkers would help his concentration.

Hirsch entered Canonero in the mile and one-eighth Stymie Handicap at Belmont on September 20, 1972, with Avila back aboard. His main opponent was that year's Kentucky Derby and Belmont win-ner Riva Ridge, who was being asked to concede thirteen pounds to Canonero. Around the far turn Canonero collared Riva Ridge and the two Kentucky Derby winners battled head and head all the way to eighth pole. It was the Preakness Stakes all over again. Canonero, as he had done to Eastern Fleet, ran Riva Ridge into the ground and drew off to a five-length victory. His time of 1:46 1/5 broke the track record by three-fifths of a second and equaled the American record.

There was still greatness in Canonero, and he proved in the Stymie that his spectacular victories in the Derby and Preakness were no fluke. But the Stymie was to be his final hurrah. Still plagued by physical problems, he finished second in an allowance race in the mud and was retired to Gainesway Farm in Lexington, Kentucky.

Baptista managed to straighten out his business but died in 1984 at age fifty-seven. Juan Arias, despite his success with Canonero, never was able to build up his stable, and his career plummeted to the point where he barely was able to eke out a living training one or two horses. Married with two children, he was forced to retire from training and take a government job, working as a technician for Consejo Nacional Electoral. But the horses were still in his blood, and on weekends he'd go to La Rinconada to visit with friends and occasionally work with the horses just to be around them, as he had as a kid.

Gustavo Avila continued to ride successfully for several years, winning numerous stakes, including the first Clasico del Caribe in Puerto Rico aboard a Venezuelan horse named Victoreado. He also rode regularly for a while in the United States. After retiring, he became involved with real estate investment, then was hired as a steward at La Rinconada. Several years later, in 2002, Arias also became a steward at La Rinconada, and he and Avila are now back together again.

Juan Arias died in August of 2021 at the age of 83, a forlorn and forgotten hero. Years earlier he said his eyes would still tear up whenever he thought of Canonero's magical journey. A young trainer Arias mentored, Gustavo Delgado, won the Kentucky Derby in 2023 with longshot Mage. After the race Delgado said, "Juan was with me at all times."

Canonero never made it as a stallion and was sent back to Venezuela in February 1981 to stand at Haras Tamanaco. The only stakes horse he sired there was El Tejano, who finished second in the group II Premio Burlesco, with none other than Gustavo Avila aboard.

"I'm saddened that Canonero was not a successful sire," Arias said. "He never really had the opportunity. Many of his foals were raised at

## Kentucky Derby
## Purse: $125,000 Added

**9th Race Churchill Downs - May 1, 1971. Ninety-seventh running Kentucky Derby.**
**Purse $125,000 added. Three-year-olds. 1 1-4 Miles. Main Track. Track: Fast.**
**Value of race $188,000. Net value to winner, $145,500 and gold trophy; second, $25,000; third, $12,500; fourth, $5,000.**

| Horse | A | Wgt | Eqp | Odds | PP | 1/4 | 1/2 | 3/4 | 1 | Str | Fin | Jockey |
|---|---|---|---|---|---|---|---|---|---|---|---|---|
| Canonero II | 3 | 126 | | f-8.70 | 12 | $16^{1}$ | $18^{5}$ | $15^{3}$ | $4^{1/2}$ | $1^{3}$ | $1^{3\frac{3}{4}}$ | G Avila |
| Jim French | 3 | 126 | b | 4.80 | 10 | $10^{h}$ | $11^{2}$ | $10^{2}$ | $7^{2}$ | $5^{1/2}$ | $2^{2}$ | A Cordero Jr |
| Bold Reason | 3 | 126 | b | 18.30 | 14 | $18^{6}$ | $16^{1/2}$ | $12^{2}$ | $9^{2}$ | $6^{2}$ | $3^{nk}$ | J Cruguet |
| Eastern Fleet | 3 | 126 | b | a-3.80 | 17 | $6^{2}$ | $3^{h}$ | $2^{1\frac{1}{2}}$ | $2^{1\frac{1}{2}}$ | $2^{h}$ | $4^{h}$ | E Maple |
| Unconscious | 3 | 126 | | 2.80 | 8 | $7^{2}$ | $6^{2}$ | $5^{1}$ | $5^{h}$ | $4^{1/2}$ | $5^{1\frac{1}{2}}$ | L Pincay Jr |
| Vegas Vic | 3 | 126 | b | 19.30 | 7 | $13^{3}$ | $13^{3}$ | $13^{1}$ | $13^{1/2}$ | $7^{1}$ | $6^{nk}$ | H Grant |
| Tribal Line | 3 | 126 | b | 80.80 | 15 | $15^{2}$ | $14^{h}$ | $17^{6}$ | $8^{1\frac{1}{2}}$ | $8^{2}$ | $7^{no}$ | D E Whited |
| Bold and Able | 3 | 126 | b | a-3.80 | 1 | $1^{h}$ | $1^{2}$ | $1^{1\frac{1}{2}}$ | $1^{h}$ | $3^{h}$ | $8^{3}$ | J Velasquez |
| List | 3 | 126 | b | 8.60 | 18 | $17^{h}$ | $17^{1/2}$ | $14^{2}$ | $14^{1\frac{1}{2}}$ | $9^{2}$ | $9^{3}$ | J Nichols |
| Twist the Axe | 3 | 126 | | c-5.10 | 11 | $9^{1/2}$ | $10^{1}$ | $7^{1}$ | $6^{1\frac{1}{2}}$ | $10^{2}$ | $10^{1\frac{1}{2}}$ | G Patterson |
| Going Straight | 3 | 126 | | 45.60 | 2 | $11^{2}$ | $8^{h}$ | $6^{h}$ | $10^{3}$ | $12^{2}$ | $11^{h}$ | O Torres |
| Royal Leverage | 3 | 126 | | b-41.60 | 5 | $19^{8}$ | $15^{2}$ | $16^{1}$ | $18^{5}$ | $11^{h}$ | $12^{2}$ | M Fromin |
| Impetuosity | 3 | 126 | | c-5.10 | 20 | $8^{1\frac{1}{2}}$ | $9^{2}$ | $8^{2}$ | $15^{1}$ | $13^{h}$ | $13^{1\frac{1}{2}}$ | E Guerin |
| Helio Rise | 3 | 126 | | 58.20 | 16 | $12^{1/2}$ | $12^{1}$ | $9^{h}$ | $11^{1}$ | $14^{1}$ | $14^{3}$ | K Knapp |
| On the Money | 3 | 126 | | b-41.60 | 9 | 20 | 20 | 20 | $17^{1/2}$ | $15^{1\frac{1}{2}}$ | $15^{1}$ | M Solomone |
| Barbizon Streak | 3 | 126 | | f-8.70 | 6 | $2^{h}$ | $5^{1}$ | $11^{1}$ | $12^{1}$ | $16^{6}$ | $16^{18}$ | D Brumfield |
| Knight Counter | 3 | 126 | b | f-8.70 | 13 | $4^{2}$ | $4^{1\frac{1}{2}}$ | $3^{1}$ | $3^{1}$ | $17^{6}$ | $17^{11}$ | M Manganello |
| Jr's Arrowhead | 3 | 126 | b | f-8.70 | 4 | $3^{h}$ | $2^{1}$ | $4^{1}$ | $16^{1\frac{1}{2}}$ | $18^{2}$ | $18^{6}$ | A Rini |
| Fourulla | 3 | 126 | | f-8.70 | 19 | $5^{h}$ | $7^{1/2}$ | $18^{3}$ | $19^{4}$ | $19^{4}$ | $19^{14}$ | D MacBeth |
| Saigon Warrior | 3 | 127 | | f-8.70 | 3 | $14^{3}$ | $19^{9}$ | $19^{5}$ | 20 | 20 | 20 | R Parrott |

f- Mutuel field.
a-Coupled, Eastern Fleet and Bold and Able; b-Royal Leverage and On the Money; c-Twist the Axe and Impetuosity.

**Off Time:** 5:43 **Time Of Race:** :23 :46⅘ 1:11⅗ 1:36⅕ 2:03⅕
**Start:** Good For All **Track:** Fast
**Equipment:** b for blinkers

**Mutuel Payoffs**

| | | | | |
|---|---|---|---|---|
| **15f** | **Canonero II** | **$19.40** | **$8.00** | **$4.20** |
| **7** | **Jim French** | | **6.20** | **4.40** |
| **8** | **Bold Reason** | | | **12.60** |

**Winner:** Canonero II, b. c. by Pretendre—Dixieland II, by Nantallah (Trained by J. Arias).
Bred by E. B. Benjamin in Ky.

**Start good. Won ridden out.**
CANONERO II, void of speed and unhurried for three-quarters, was forced to come to the extreme outside to launch his bid upon leaving the backstretch, continued to circle his field entering the stretch to take command with a bold rush in the upper stretch and was under intermittent urging to prevail. JIM FRENCH, allowed to settle in stride, moved up along the inside when launching his bid on the second turn, was forced to come out between horses entering the stretch, commenced lugging in to brush with BARBIZON STREAK, continued gamely to move through close quarters in midstretch, but could not reach the winner. JIM FRENCH came back with a cut on the coronet band of his right rear foot. BOLD REASON, badly outrun for six furlongs, moved between horses until forced to steady when blocked in the upper stretch, dropped to the inside when clear and finished with good courage. EASTERN FLEET, away alertly to gain a forward position along the inside, moved through in slightly close quarters leaving the backstretch, moved to the fore between calls in the upper stretch, commenced drifting out in the closing drive and gave way willingly. UNCONSCIOUS, never far back while along the inner railing, continued to save ground while moving into serious contention on the final turn, came out for the drive and had little left when the real test came. BOLD AND ABLE was sent to the fore at once, bore out entering the first turn, came back to the inside when clear to make the pace to the top of the stretch, at which point he dropped back steadily. LIST failed to enter contention while closing some ground in the late stages. TWIST THE AXE, in hand early, moved up along the outside after three-quarters to loom boldly on the final turn but could not sustain his bid. IMPETUOSITY, breaking smartly from his outside positioon, continued slightly wide to midway down the backstretch where he was dropped in to move up between horses, was forced to check sharply when JR'S ARROWHEAD dropped over at the half-mile ground, losing his action, and failed to recover when clear. BARBIZON STREAK, away in good order, was caught in close quarters entering the first turn, continued slightly wide and commenced dropping back after five furlongs. KNIGHT COUNTER was bumped and forced out entering the first turn. JR'S ARROWHEAD came away alertly to gain a striking position along the outside, commenced lugging in at the half-mile ground and dropped back steadily. FOURULLA bore out badly entering the first turn.
**Overweight—Saigon, 1 pound. Scratched—Sole Mio.**

**Owners:** (1) E Caibett; (2) F J Caldwell; (3) W A Levin; (4) Calumet Farm; (5) A A Seeligson Jr; (6) Betty Sechrest-C Fritz; (7) J E-T A Grissom; (8) Calumet Farm; (9) Mrs J W Brown; (10) Pastorale Stable; (11) Donamire Farm; (12) P Teinowitz; (13) W P Rosso; (14) R W-R T Wilson Jr; (15) Teinowitz-Schmidt; (16) Mrs H J Udouj; (17) R Huffman; (18) Walnut Hill Farm; (19) A H Sullivan; (20) C M Day

King Ranch in Texas, and that wasn't the best place to raise a young horse. And the quality of mares he was bred to was not appropriate for a horse they expected so much from."

On November 11, 1981, Canonero was found dead in his stall, the victim of an apparent heart attack. By then the magnificent decade of the seventies was history, with Secretariat, Forego, Seattle Slew, Affirmed, Alydar, and Spectacular Bid all stamping their place in the record books. But few remembered that it was Canonero who paved the way for these media stars and the resurgence of the sport.

By the time of his death, the cries of "Viva Canonero" had faded to a mere whisper, and the horse who had electrified the racing world like no other before him had slipped quietly back into the obscurity from which he had come.

But those who were there to witness the frenzy of that unforgettable spring will never forget Canonero. *Washington Post* columnist and handicapper Andrew Beyer wrote: "Even in a decade that was to produce such horses as Secretariat, Affirmed, and Spectacular Bid, there was no Triple Crown series that evoked such passions as that of 1971."

Canonero's Derby and Preakness trophies were given to La Rinconada, but they are not even exhibited anywhere. As the years pass by and new generations of racing fans emerge, the name of Canonero drifts deeper into memory, as do his amazing feats. The legendary sportswriter Red Smith wrote that the ninety-seventh Kentucky Derby "was won by a colt in a plain brown wrapper." In many ways he was correct, but the truth is, there was never anything plain about Canonero II.

*By Steve Haskin*

# Stand Up Guy
## (Iron Liege, 1957)

SOME SPORTING EVENTS live in popular memory because of heroic achievements — the 1980 victory of the U.S. Olympic hockey team over Russia or Kirk Gibson's improbable home run off Dennis Eckersley in the 1988 World Series.

Others are remembered because of a fierce rivalry — Ohio State versus Michigan for the Big Ten football crown or Affirmed versus Alydar in the classic 1978 Triple Crown races.

Then there are those contests whose very mention brings to mind a dreadful mistake — California center Roy Riegels running sixty-five yards the wrong way with a recovered fumble in the 1929 Rose Bowl or the ground ball trickling between Bill Buckner's legs in Game Six of the 1986 World Series.

Sadly, the 1957 Kentucky Derby falls into the last category. The eighty-third renewal of the Run for the Roses will be remembered as the year jockey Bill Shoemaker misjudged the finish line, costing Gallant Man a seemingly sure victory.

The race certainly didn't shape up that way, either in prospect or in retrospect. As Derby Day approached, the race was expected to be a classic among classics, with that year's three-year-olds being an unusually fast and talented crop of Thoroughbreds. In fact, the foal crop of 1954 is widely regarded as one of the best ever. Of the ten main Derby contenders, two later would be included among the top twenty horses of the twentieth century. Those two — Bold Ruler and Round Table — as well as Gallant Man and Iron Liege, would go on to live in the pedigrees of future stakes performers.

The various contenders had taken turns in the limelight as two-year-olds, and none had really established dominance during the run-up to the Derby. What they had established was a reputation for talent and speed.

Federal Hill had set a world record of 1:15 for six and a half furlongs at Gulfstream Park in March. Round Table broke the Keeneland record for nine furlongs by finishing the Blue Grass Stakes in 1:47 2/5. Gen. Duke matched the world record for nine furlongs, winning the Florida Derby in 1:46 4/5. Bold Ruler set a Hialeah track record of 1:47 in the Flamingo but, despite that effort, only beat Gen. Duke by a nose. Bold Ruler also set a track record in winning the Wood Memorial at Jamaica in 1:48 4/5.

Gallant Man equaled the track record for six furlongs at Tropical Park on January 3, defeating Gen. Duke by six lengths. And Iron Liege

**Gallant Man with Bill Shoemaker up**

had defeated Gen. Duke, his stablemate, twice, by more than two lengths in the Dallas Park Purse at Hialeah on February 9, setting a track record for one and one-sixteenth miles, and in the High Hope Purse at Keeneland, equaling the track record for seven furlongs.

*Chicago Sun-Times* Turf writer Joe Agrella looked over the accomplishments of the prospective starters and commented, "Yep, this Derby is spelled s-p-e-e-d."

But the quality of the competitors is only one factor in any race, and sometimes circumstances can overshadow raw ability. And as the players worked their way toward Churchill Downs and their once-in-a-lifetime chance at Derby immortality, some clues began to surface indicating this Run for the Roses would be about more than which horse reached the finish line first.

First, there was the little matter of who would ride Gallant Man.

In 1955 trainer John Nerud had purchased a group of horses from the Aga Khan for Texan Ralph Lowe. A small colt at just 15 hands, the British-bred Gallant Man had been thrown in as part of the group, despite the fact the colt was sired by Prix de l'Arc de Triomphe winner Migoli and was out of Irish Oaks and Irish One Thousand Guineas winner Majideh.

At two Gallant Man had won just three races from seven starts. He started off the new year with a bang, with his Tropical Park performance and a solid score in the Hibiscus Stakes at Hialeah, in which both Federal Hill and Round Table ran unplaced. But then in the Bahamas Stakes, Gallant Man finished fourth behind Bold Ruler, Gen. Duke, and Federal Hill, and he was fourth again in the April 6 Swift Stakes at Jamaica.

In his final Derby prep Gallant Man finished second by a nose to Bold Ruler in the Wood Memorial at Jamaica, with regular rider, John Choquette, aboard. However, stewards at Jamaica suspended Choquette for rough riding several days after the Wood. In those days stewards' rulings usually stood, with no exceptions for stakes races or long court battles. So Choquette was off Gallant Man and out of the Derby picture.

**Iron Liege gallops before the Derby**

SKEETS MEADORS

Nerud had selected Choquette, but according to Shoemaker in his autobiography *Shoemaker, America's Greatest Jockey*, co-authored by *Daily Racing Form* columnist, author, and broadcast commentator Barney Nagler, Ralph Lowe had wanted Shoemaker to ride Gallant Man from the beginning. Nerud told Lowe, "You want another jockey, you can get another trainer, too," and the owner backed down, allowing Choquette to keep the mount.

Only when Choquette was suspended did Nerud look elsewhere for a rider for Gallant Man, Shoemaker said. And then he turned to California because too many of the East Coast jockeys had declined the assignment when Gallant Man first started out. "Nerud had a long memory," Shoemaker said. "So when he needed a rider for Gallant Man for the 1957 Derby, he went right to the phone and called the jocks' room at Hollywood Park and asked me if I was available to ride Gallant Man. 'Betcha I am,' I said."

Nerud's selection of Shoemaker to replace Choquette for the Derby turned into a nightmare for owner Lowe — literally. With the switch apparently weighing heavily on his subconscious, Lowe dreamed two nights before the Derby that Shoemaker had pulled the colt up before the wire. Lowe reported his dream to trainer John Nerud, and Nerud said he repeated the story to Shoemaker over dinner the night before the Derby.

According to contemporary accounts, the trainer said he told the jockey, "Whatever you do, Willie, ride the horse out around the turn. He's fit. Ride past the wire."

No one outside that inner circle knew about Lowe's premonition as Derby Day approached. But another harbinger of Derby fortunes was out there for all to see in a brand-new publication called *Sports Illustrated*.

Preparing for its first editions, *Sports Illustrated* had sent a reporter and photographer to Calumet Farm on March 20, 1954, hoping to catch the delivery of a foal that might become a Derby contender. The foal whose birth they caught shortly after midnight on March 21 was Iron Liege.

Through the next three years *Sports Illustrated* followed the colt's progress, returning to Calumet to photograph him at various stages of development. In its February 25, 1957, issue — more than two months before Derby Day — *Sports Illustrated* published a photo essay on Iron Liege, headlined: "The Baby Started at 9,066 to 1," referring to the 9,067 registered foals of 1954.

The article concluded with the following: "He has yet to penetrate the threshold of greatness, and may never do so. But Iron Liege is already a successful horse. The 9,066-to-1 baby is now a man, and only a 15-to-1 shot for next May's Kentucky Derby."

But the magazine was new, and few people paid much attention to its experimental coverage of the longshot colt.

As the players gathered in Louisville, it appeared Calumet Farm had the upper hand with its entry of Gen. Duke and Iron Liege. Gen. Duke and Wheatley Stable's Bold Ruler had taken turns beating one another in Florida early in the year. Gen. Duke then shot to the top of

KINETIC CORP.

After Bill Shoemaker stands up in the stirrups, costing Gallant Man (outside) momentum in the final yards, Iron Liege holds on to win at the wire

the Derby list with his world-record-tying Florida Derby performance.

But Gen. Duke bruised his left front foot while finishing second to Federal Hill in the April 30 Derby Trial, casting doubt on whether the Calumet first-stringer would even make the Derby. Meanwhile, Iron Liege finished fifth in the Trial, dropping his stock as a Derby contender and further darkening Calumet's once-bright chances.

Gen. Duke's injury at first did not appear too serious. Trainer Jimmy Jones said his colt had experienced a similar problem after the Florida Derby but had worked through it as he continued training. Still, Jones was concerned enough to watch his star colt carefully and agonize about whether Gen. Duke could overcome the problem in time to run in the Derby. While he awaited the arrival of special bar shoes from California to relieve the pressure on the sore foot, Jones applied hot water and poultices and hoped for the best.

For days conflicting reports emanated from the Churchill Downs backstretch. Some had it that the colt was okay and training well; others, that he continued to feel the effects of the nagging injury and was not traveling well. Jones' own confidence in Gen. Duke seemed to waver from day to day through Derby week, fueling the public uncertainty.

The decision about whether to race the colt would have been tough under any circumstances, but these were not just any circumstances. This was Calumet, and this was the Kentucky Derby. Calumet, with all due deference to Iron Liege, was expecting Gen. Duke to complete the stable's comeback to honor and glory after several "down" years in the early and mid-1950s.

Calumet, under the ownership of Warren Wright, won its first Derby in 1941 with Whirlaway. Pensive won the 1944 renewal, toting Calumet's devil's red-and-blue colors. After a second in 1945 and a third in 1947, Calumet sent out the one-two finishers in the 1948 running — Citation and Coaltown — and backed that up by winning the 1949 Derby with Ponder. In 1952, with Warren Wright's widow, Lucille Parker Wright, at the helm, Calumet's Hill Gail wore the roses on Derby Day.

But, by its own high standards, the stable had been in a bit of a slump since 1952, both in the Kentucky Derby and in general. The down period

JIM RAFTERY/TURFOTOS

**Gen. Duke captures the Florida Derby with Bold Ruler second and Iron Liege third**

coincided with a decision to shift its focus of racing operations to the West Coast. In 1954 Calumet dropped to fourth on the list of leading owners by winnings. It was the first time the farm had been out of the top three in that category since 1939. In 1955 Calumet dropped to eighth place on the list and abandoned its move to California.

While 1956 was a rebound year — Calumet was back on top of the earnings list and Fabius was second in the Derby and provided Calumet with its fifth win in the Preakness — 1957 was viewed as the year the farm would regain Derby Day glory.

And if those expectations weren't enough pressure on Jones, there was another consideration: Gen. Duke was sired by Calumet's own "franchise" stallion, Bull Lea.

Bull Lea was the linchpin in the Calumet operation. Benefiting from the quality of the farm's broodmare band, the staunch stallion sired 377 foals, fifty-eight of them stakes winners. They included the likes of Armed, Bewitch, Citation, Coaltown, Two Lea, and Hill Gail. He also sired Iron Liege, and if both ran, Calumet would have a chance for another one-two homebred Derby finish.

Calumet had already seen its 1956 juvenile champion Barbizon, who had won the Garden State Stakes at two, knocked off the Derby trail because of a virus. With question marks about Iron Liege's form, eliminating Gen. Duke from the race would significantly hurt the resurgent farm's chances to capture more Derby glory.

So, a great deal was riding on Jones' evaluation of an equine foot as April turned to May and the first Saturday loomed.

Jimmy Jones, christened Horace Allyn Jones, himself had the breeding to make the right decision for the right reasons. A son of Calumet's long-time and legendary trainer Ben Jones, Jimmy Jones had been around top horses all his life. The father-son team arrived at Calumet in 1939 and during the pair's long tenure Calumet reigned as the nation's leading owner twelve times and as leading breeder fourteen times. Among the numerous champions Jimmy Jones trained for Calumet were Horses of the Year Armed and Citation.

A horseman to his very marrow, Jones in the end knew what he had to do.

"It's not fair to the public to run him if he's not 100 percent fit," Jones said after blowing out Gen. Duke on Derby Day morning. Although the colt covered a quarter-mile in :24, Jones said he appeared to be favoring the injured foot.

With Gen. Duke out of the field, Bold Ruler became the favorite and that choice seemed more than logical. A son of the British-bred sire Nasrullah, who would sire ninety-nine stakes winners, Bold Ruler was out of a highly successful stakes-winning mare, Miss Disco.

Despite some physical problems, including a number of minor injuries, Bold Ruler won his first five starts. He later won the Futurity at Belmont Park but struggled in his last two races of the year and lost the two-year-old title to Calumet's Barbizon. Racing for the Wheatley Stable of Mrs. Henry Carnegie Phipps of New York, Bold Ruler won the Flamingo at Hialeah and finished second to Gen. Duke in the Florida Derby before winning the Wood Memorial en route to Churchill Downs. His regular rider was five-time Derby-winning jockey Eddie Arcaro.

Bold Ruler's eighty-two-year-old trainer, Sunny Jim Fitzsimmons, seemed more interested in discussing the weather than in discussing his colt mid-week before the Derby. But, led back to the topic while talking to reporters outside Barn 16, he allowed, "Bold Ruler? Oh, he's ready." The colt proved it by breezing six furlongs between races on Wednesday of Derby week in 1:11 1/5.

While Bold Ruler emerged as the favorite after Gen. Duke's declaration from the race, Kerr Stable's Round Table also was drawing a lot of attention. Bred by A.B. (Bull) Hancock Jr.'s Claiborne Farm, Round Table was by Princequillo out of Knight's Daughter. (In one of those racetrack coincidences that enliven the sport, Round Table and Bold Ruler were both foaled on the same day at Claiborne Farm.)

Claiborne Farm had sold a majority interest in Round Table to

MIKE SIRICO/NYRA

**Bold Ruler (inside) edges Gallant Man in the Wood Memorial**

SKEETS MEADORS

**Ben (left) and Jimmy Jones lead Iron Liege into the winner's circle**

Oklahoma oil man Travis Kerr early in the colt's three-year-old season for a reported $145,000. That price reflected what had been a promising but not stellar juvenile career. During the summer of his two-year-old year, Round Table had won only a single race in four tries on the Chicago circuit. Having improved as the year wound down, he finished second in the Hyde Park Stakes at Arlington and traveled south to Keeneland, where he won the Breeders' Futurity in an upset.

As a three-year-old, Round Table finished third in the Santa Anita Derby, then later in the spring won the Bay Meadows Derby. He made a statement in winning the Blue Grass Stakes by six lengths in record time at Keeneland. But some analysts feared he preferred a surface harder than the sandy loam of Churchill Downs.

While Bold Ruler, Gallant Man, and Round Table were clearly the pick of the Derby field after Gen. Duke's defection, some saw the Derby

Trial winner and likely pacesetter Federal Hill as having a chance to hang on for the win. Only two years earlier Swaps had led all of the way to upset Nashua. And two years prior to that, Dark Star used the lead and a trouble-free trip to post a huge upset of Native Dancer.

Federal Hill had shown little liking for distances over a mile, much less the Derby's mile and a quarter. But his trainer, Milt Rieser, said the Cosmic Bomb colt's penchant for the Churchill Downs surface would make the difference. "Federal Hill likes this track," Rieser told reporters days before the Run for the Roses. "He's run at Churchill Downs twice and won easily." In addition to the Derby Trial win, he also won the Kentucky Jockey Club Stakes as a juvenile.

With Gen. Duke now out of the race, Iron Liege went into the Derby as Calumet Farm's lone entrant. His fifth-place finish in the Trial remained fresh in everyone's mind, and questions about his ability still abounded despite an earlier second-place finish in the Fountain of Youth and thirds in both the Flamingo and the Florida Derby.

Young jockey Bill Hartack would be aboard Iron Liege for the Kentucky Derby. Hartack was making only his second start in the race. He had finished second in 1956 on Calumet Farm's Fabius after leading into deep stretch.

The other runners were longshots, enticing for the punters who pick by names or by stabbing their programs with a hatpin, hoping for a winner at a long price. Tennessee Wright, trainer of Shan Pac, who went to the post at odds of nearly 47-1 and would finish last, summed up his horse's chances and those of the other lesser-lights of the field: "This colt was born in the wrong year. Too many tough horses in this Derby."

The weather was cool and the track was fast on May 4 as the nine starters loaded into the Churchill Downs starting gate for the seventh race on the nine-race program.

The crowd had made Bold Ruler the favorite, at just better than even money. Round Table was second choice at 3.60-1, with Gallant Man right behind at 3.70-1. Iron Liege went to the post at 8-1.

At 4:32 p.m., the bell rang and, as expected, Federal Hill, from post position two, was the first to answer. With William Carstens up, the 8-1 shot opened a one and a half-length lead after a half-mile, running the first quarter in :23 3/5 and the half in :47.

At the half Bold Ruler was second, Iron Liege was third, and Round Table was fourth. Shoemaker had Gallant Man well in hand and was saving ground in seventh position. With a mile gone and just two furlongs to the wire, Federal Hill was hanging on in front in 1:36 4/5. But now Iron Liege was breathing down his neck, with Bold Ruler in third and Round Table still fourth. Shoemaker and Gallant Man had begun their move but remained in fifth.

At this point in the race, it became apparent that Rieser had been a bit optimistic in predicting Federal Hill could get a distance of ground, even on a friendly track. As the front-runner tired, Hartack sent Iron Liege up to challenge for the lead. The rivals straightened out into the long stretch run with the crowd on its feet and in full voice. Midway down the lane Iron Liege had the advantage.

Shoemaker, meanwhile, had been moving boldly with Gallant Man from his ground-saving position. As the field pounded down the stretch, Gallant Man began moving inexorably toward Iron Liege and appeared ready to go by him to win the race.

What happened next was so subtle that it wasn't apparent to everyone watching the race. Approaching the sixteenth pole, Shoemaker stood in his irons and seemed about to pull Gallant Man up. Having realized his mistake, the jockey immediately sat back down and began scrubbing on his colt again, but it was too late. Gallant Man had lost precious momentum, and Iron Liege had enough left to push his nose in front at the wire. It seemed Ralph Lowe's nightmare had indeed become a reality.

While the Churchill crowd might not have realized immediately what had happened, several racing officials did. So did Lowe, who stood in shock.

"A furious Nerud rushed down to the track to confront Shoemaker," Steve Haskin recounts in a chapter about the trainer in the book *Dr. Fager*. "All he wanted was for the rider to admit his mistake and not blame the horse. 'If he'd said something about the horse, I was gonna hit him with the f----in' (field) glasses,' Nerud was quoted as saying. But as soon as Shoemaker saw Nerud, he said, 'I'm sorry, John. I made a mistake.' The incident was over."

But Shoemaker's error became part of the official record. *Daily Racing Form* chart caller Don Fair wrote in the chart footnotes that Gallant Man "moved up determinedly in the early stretch, reached the lead between calls and was going stoutly when his rider misjudged the finish line and he could not overtake Iron Liege when back on stride."

It was the closest Kentucky Derby finish since 1933 when Brokers Tip beat Head Play by a nose in a roughly run stretch battle.

Round Table, who got to within a length of the lead in the final furlong, couldn't maintain his bid and finished third, two and three-quarters lengths back. Bold Ruler raced well off the rail through the ten furlongs and could do no better than fourth, three lengths behind Round Table. Arcaro later said he held the colt too long and discouraged him from making a run to the lead. Bold Ruler was known to have an extraordinarily sensitive mouth, due to an accident he had suffered as a yearling, and resented being held.

**Iron Liege in the Derby winner's circle with Bill Hartack up**

Federal Hill was fifth after setting the pace, followed by the four extreme longshots — Indian Creek, Mister Jive, Better Bee, and Shan Pac. None of those four ever came close to being a factor in the race.

The time was 2:02 1/5, unremarkable given the previous record-setting quickness of the main combatants. At the time, the Churchill Downs and the Kentucky Derby record for a mile and a quarter was Whirlaway's 2:01 2/5, posted in 1941.

The story of the eighty-third Run for the Roses, however, quickly became Shoemaker's error in judgment. How could a jockey make such a terrible and costly blunder in the biggest race of the year? The Shoe went through stages in explaining the boner.

Initially, he said only that he wasn't sure who had won as Iron Liege and Gallant Man flashed under the wire.

The next day, with criticism raining down on Shoemaker, trainer John Nerud blamed Churchill Downs, saying The Shoe "rode a masterful race … I blame the racetrack, not Shoemaker. They got no business putting the finish wire down near the first turn. And all those poles are the same color."

By the time Shoemaker got around to discussing the matter in his autobiography, the jockey had accepted the responsibility for his action but wasn't making a big deal out of the mistake.

Discussing the time he replaced Ron Franklin on Spectacular Bid after The Bid lost the Belmont Stakes, Shoemaker said, "Anybody can make a mistake riding a race. Remember, I misjudged the finish line and threw away a Derby once. Arcaro, about as great a rider as any in the twentieth century, eased a horse a mile too soon and was disqualified in a race at Pimlico. It happens. It just happens."

Later in the same volume Shoemaker writes about the 1957 Derby, "I might as well come right out with it. That was the Derby I bobbled. I was riding Gallant Man and I mistook the finish line and stood up in the irons. It probably cost me the race. Hartack beat me by a nose on Iron Liege. People never forget to remind me about my mistake. Wherever I go, they ask me to tell them about the time I goofed on Gallant Man. When they ask, I tell it straight. I made a horrible mistake."

Nonetheless, corroborating evidence exists for Nerud's contention that the Churchill finish can be confusing. A similar incident occurred in the 1946 Derby, won by Assault. In that seventy-second renewal jockey Job Dean Jessup pulled up Hampden sharply after misjudging the finish line, and according to the chart footnotes, the colt "came again when roused but could not better his position," finishing third, just a head behind Spy Song.

Those who blamed Shoemaker pointed to his own similar mistake in 1956, when a misjudged finish cost Swaps a victory at Hollywood Park.

Shoemaker's and Nerud's attitudes notwithstanding, Lowe's forgiveness for the blunder was swift. He gave Shoe a new Chrysler and five thousand dollars in gratitude for his efforts. The jockey responded by riding Gallant Man to victory five weeks later in the Belmont Stakes.

The stewards were not in such a forgiving mood. Steward Lincoln Plaut, who detected Shoemaker's miscue and may have tipped the *Daily Racing Form*'s Fair to it, handed the jockey a fifteen-day suspension. Ironically, Shoemaker had gotten the mount because of a suspension and wound up suspended himself.

The Calumet connections gather for the trophy presentation

The action was controversial and met with some criticism. But Plaut defended the suspension to the Louisville *Courier-Journal* in a story published May 9, 1957, calling Shoemaker's actions "gross negligence." Without referring to Shoemaker's ride as a mistake, Plaut said, "The people didn't come out to see a horse that a jockey wasn't going to ride out. The public must have some kind of explanation for such an action."

In his autobiography, Shoemaker defends the right of stewards to police jockeys and complains not about the fifteen days but about the attitude of the officials who handed them down.

Discussing the suspension that prevented Choquette from riding in the Derby, Shoemaker said, "In those days, when the stewards suspended a jockey, he stayed suspended. These days the stewards are different. When they take action against a rider, he goes to court and gets an injunction and keeps riding. This might be a good thing in some cases, but it weakens the power of the stewards."

His suspension for the Gallant Man ride was delivered by telegram, Shoemaker said. "It said that under the circumstances, they had to suspend me for fifteen days. I got pissy. So did John Nerud. The suspension itself didn't bother me. I was a pro and pros weren't supposed to goof. What bothered me was the way they did it."

The unnatural finish of the 1957 Derby masked the fact that its top contestants were among the best in recent history. Iron Liege's name went into the Derby record books. But the beaten contenders went on to far greater glory than the horse who had beaten them on the first Saturday in May.

Iron Liege wound up his three-year-old season with eight wins in seventeen starts and earnings of $312,625. He raced eight times as a four-year-old, winning only once. He didn't rate a mention in *Thoroughbred Champions: Top 100 Racehorses of the 20th Century*, as compiled by a panel of experts for *The Blood-Horse* magazine. Iron Liege was retired to stud in France and later sent to Japan. He did little as a sire in either country.

Gallant Man ranks thirty-sixth in that listing and undoubtedly

## Kentucky Derby
## Purse: $125,000 Added

**6th Race Churchill Downs - May 4, 1957. Eighty-third running Kentucky Derby.**
**Purse $125,000 added. Three-year-olds. 1 1-4 Miles. Main Track. Track: Fast.**
**Gross value $152,050. Net value to winner, $107,950 and gold trophy; second, $25,000; third, $12,500; fourth, $5,000.**

| Horse | A | Wgt | Eqp | Odds | PP | St | 1/2 | 3/4 | 1 | Str | Fin | Jockey |
|---|---|---|---|---|---|---|---|---|---|---|---|---|
| Iron Liege | 3 | 126 | w | 8.40 | 6 | 4 | $3^{3}$ | $2^{1½}$ | $2^{1½}$ | $1^{½}$ | $1^{no}$ | W Hartack |
| Gallant Man | 3 | 126 | w | 3.70 | 4 | 6 | $7^{2}$ | $7^{1}$ | $5^{½}$ | $3^{½}$ | $2^{2¾}$ | W Shoemaker |
| Round Table | 3 | 126 | wb | 3.60 | 3 | 5 | $4^{3}$ | $4^{3}$ | $4^{2}$ | $4^{h}$ | $3^{3}$ | R Neves |
| Bold Ruler | 3 | 126 | w | 1.20 | 7 | 3 | $2^{h}$ | $3^{1½}$ | $3^{½}$ | $5^{3}$ | $4^{1¼}$ | E Arcaro |
| Federal Hill | 3 | 126 | wb | 7.90 | 2 | 1 | $1^{1½}$ | $1^{½}$ | $1^{h}$ | $2^{h}$ | $5^{¾}$ | W Carstens |
| Indian Creek | 3 | 126 | wb | 73.10 | 5 | 7 | $6^{2½}$ | $6^{½}$ | $7^{3}$ | $7^{3}$ | $6^{1}$ | G Taniguchi |
| Mister Jive | 3 | 126 | wb | 55.90 | 1 | 2 | $5^{3}$ | $5^{2½}$ | $6^{½}$ | $6^{½}$ | $7^{3½}$ | H Woodhouse |
| Better Bee | 3 | 126 | w | 42.40 | 9 | 9 | 9 | 9 | $8^{3}$ | $8^{6}$ | $8^{10}$ | J Adams |
| Shan Pac | 3 | 126 | wb | 46.50 | 8 | 8 | $8^{½}$ | $8^{½}$ | 9 | 9 | 9 | J R Adams |

**Off Time:** 4:32 **Time Of Race:** :23⅗ :47 1:11⅕ 1:36⅘ 2:02⅕
**Start:** Good For All **Track:** Fast
**Equipment:** w for whip; b for blinkers

**Mutuel Payoffs**

| | | | | |
|---|---|---|---|---|
| **1A** | **Iron Liege** | **$18.80** | **$9.40** | **$6.20** |
| **5** | **Gallant Man** | | **5.00** | **4.00** |
| **4** | **Round Table** | | | **4.00** |

**Winner:** Iron Liege, b. c. by Bull Lea—Iron Maiden, by War Admiral (Trained by H. A. Jones).
Bred by Calumet Farm in Ky.

**Start good. Won driving; second and third the same.**
IRON LIEGE, away alertly, saved ground while racing nearest FEDERAL HILL to the mile, took command during the drive and, responding to strong handling, held GALLANT MAN safe but won with little left. GALLANT MAN, in hand and saving ground to the last three-eighths mile, moved up determinedly in the early stretch, reached the lead between calls and was going stoutly when his rider misjudged the finish and he could not overtake IRON LIEGE when back on stride. ROUND TABLE, well placed and racing evenly to the stretch, closed willingly under punishment but could not reach the leaders. BOLD RULER, a sharp factor from the outset but racing well out in the track, failed to stay when set down through the stretch. FEDERAL HILL took command at once, set the pace until inside the stretch, then gave way when challenged by IRON LIEGE. INDIAN CREEK was never prominent and had no mishap. MISTER JIVE could not keep up. BETTER BEE was never dangerous. SHAN PAC was overmatched.
**Scratched—Gen. Duke, 126.**

**Owners:** (1) Calumet Farm; (2) R Lowe; (3) Kerr Stable; (4) Wheatley Stable; (5) C Lussky; (6) Mrs A L Rice; (6) J L Applebaum; (7) W S Miller; (8) T A Grissom
©EQUIBASE

would have rated higher had he not faced such tough competition throughout his racing career. Gallant Man skipped the Preakness after the Derby disaster but then won the Belmont Stakes by eight lengths, with Bold Ruler running third. His time of 2:26 3/5 stood as the Belmont record until Secretariat came along.

Overall, Gallant Man won eight of fourteen starts at three, with $298,280 in earnings. In three years of racing, he won fourteen of twenty-six starts and earned $510,355. He won at distances from five furlongs to two miles. At stud he sired fifty-two stakes winners and was the broodmare sire of ninety-one stakes winners, including the 1980 Kentucky Derby winner Genuine Risk.

Bold Ruler's career was even better. He ranks nineteenth on the Top

100 list. After his flat effort in the Derby, Bold Ruler won the Preakness. He flopped in the Belmont but then went on a tear that earned him Horse of the Year and champion three-year-old colt honors. At four he won five of seven starts, carrying as much as 135 pounds and giving up as much as twenty pounds to his rivals. In three years on the track, he won twenty-three of thirty-three races. He was champion sprinter in 1958.

At stud Bold Ruler would have been a fabulous success even if he hadn't sired Secretariat. He led the American sire list a phenomenal eight times, had eighty-two stakes winners, and is the broodmare sire of 119 stakes winners, including seven champions.

And Round Table did better yet, ranking seventeenth.

After the Derby he was shipped to California where he finished second in the Californian Stakes, competing against older horses. He then went on to win eleven straight races, including the Hollywood Gold Cup, the American Derby at Arlington Park, the United Nations Handicap, and the Hawthorne Gold Cup. The string ended with a defeat in the Trenton Handicap (to Bold Ruler; Gallant Man was second), but Round Table ended the year with a victory in the Malibu Stakes. He won fifteen of twenty-two starts as a three-year-old.

In four years of racing, Round Table won forty-three of his sixty-six starts and placed in thirteen for fifty-six top three finishes. He earned $1,749,869. He was Horse of the Year in 1958; champion grass horse in 1957, 1958, and 1959; and champion older horse in 1958 and 1959.

He, too, was a rousing success in the breeding shed, siring eighty-three stakes winners. He is the broodmare sire of 125 stakes winners.

So, while the 1957 Derby itself will be remembered alongside "wrong way" runs and wayward ground balls, its key participants will live forever among the immortals of their sport.

*By Robert Kieckhefer*

# The Rivalry
## (Affirmed, 1978)

CALL IT A SUMMIT MEETING; call it a showdown; call it a rumble in the Bluegrass.

Whatever you call it, each Kentucky Derby shares with its predecessors the uniqueness of being first: first race in the Triple Crown series and certainly the only time each horse has a chance to achieve racing immortality by sweeping the series; first time for its competitors to go a mile and a quarter; first time for the entire field to carry 126 pounds apiece; first — and often only — meeting of all the leading three-year-olds in training.

Small wonder, then, that the Derby is the most glamorous, sought-after race in Thoroughbred racing. For months, often stretching well back into the previous year, a small army of owners, breeders, trainers, and jockeys have been thinking the unthinkable: Do we have a Kentucky Derby winner in the barn? On the first Saturday of each May, all the gathering hopes, dreams, and scarcely suppressed expectations of those whose horses make it to the Derby are on the line, accompanied by fluttering hearts, sweaty palms, and enough nervous energy to light up most of Louisville.

Yes, every Derby is a summit meeting, but there are those rare occasions when all the pre-race buildup, all the hysteria, all the hype turn out to be the real thing, and racing fans get to witness a Derby for the ages, one whose outcome will find its way into the enduring chronicles of the sport.

Such a Derby was contested in 1978, a year when there were two colts whose star qualities obscured everything else around them, and

KINETIC CORP.

**Affirmed and Steve Cauthen after the Run for the Roses**

made the 104th running of the Kentucky Derby a rivalry in which two amazing racehorses raised their head-to-head competition to a new, unparalleled level.

Racing fans everywhere — not to mention racing insiders — had figured out that the 1978 Derby would come down to a two-horse duel, and everyone knew the names of the duelists: Affirmed and Alydar.

From their earliest two-year-old appearances these two chestnut colts had demonstrated exceptional class and consistency, brushing aside virtually all their competition, except for each other. Each had the pedigree and conformation to suggest that he could be anything as a racehorse.

Affirmed, a Florida-bred, was a product of the highly successful Harbor View Farm racing and breeding operation of financier Louis Wolfson.

The handsome, elegantly attired Wolfson had acquired a significant fortune and a reputation as one of America's foremost corporate raiders. A man with the financial savvy and audacity to challenge orthodox business practices, he won more often than he lost.

In the late 1950s Wolfson blended those talents with his horseplayer's passion for Thoroughbred racing and quickly became a force in the racing game, establishing his farm near Ocala, Florida, while racing primarily in New York. In 1960 his racing stable, featuring stakes stars like Francis S. and Garwol, ranked third in the national owners' standings and appeared among the national leaders annually through much of the '60s. In 1965 Harbor View raced Horse of the Year Roman Brother, an exceptional handicap horse. During the 1960s Harbor View also rose quickly to prominence as a breeding entity, achieving high ranking in industry breeding statistics as well.

The most notable horse Wolfson campaigned during this period was Raise a Native, a powerful chestnut son of the great Native Dancer. An early maturing colt, Raise a Native was so dominant in his first four starts, all easy victories, that many experienced horsemen were convinced he might be comparable to his sire as a racehorse.

An injury ended Raise a Native's racing career before he could realize his full potential. He began his stud career at Kentucky-based Spendthrift Farm, where breeders, including his owner, quickly patronized him. Wolfson sent several of his best mares to the young stallion, including the Alfred Vanderbilt-bred Exclusive, a stakes-producing daughter of 1942 Kentucky Derby-Belmont winner Shut Out.

From the mating, Exclusive foaled a colt named Exclusive Native, who performed at such a high level for Harbor View's racing outfit during an injury-plagued career that at the end of his three-year-old season he joined his sire at Spendthrift.

Exclusive Native was an early success at stud, siring among others the high-quality stakes winner Our Native, out of a daughter of champion older horse Crafty Admiral. Our Native's racing achievements led Wolfson to send another Crafty Admiral mare, Won't Tell You, to Exclusive Native in 1974. Won't Tell You's female family had been more solid than scintillating for several generations, producing a string of modest winners — "hard knockers" as they are often known to racetrackers — but nothing of exceptional merit. However, Lou Wolfson's hunch about the Exclusive Native-Crafty Admiral affinity was about to pay off spectacularly with the birth of Won't Tell You's next baby, a colt named Affirmed.

Alydar was also a product of one

Affirmed holds a fast-closing Alydar safe at the wire for the Derby win; (inset) Steve Cauthen and Affirmed receive their roses

KINETIC CORP.; (INSET) MILT TOBY

76

of horse racing's "blue hen" nurseries. But his birthplace, Calumet Farm, was already a racing powerhouse when Lou Wolfson was still in the early stages of building his business empire, long before Harbor View was a gleam in his eye.

Calumet had been a successful Standardbred farm under founder

William Monroe Wright, but his son Warren was determined to make a splash in the Thoroughbred world, and by the 1940s the farm was sitting atop a tidal wave.

The Calumet horses, bearing devil's red-and-blue silks, seemed to win major stakes events wherever they pleased. In the 1940s, the stable captured four Kentucky Derbies (Whirlaway, 1941; Pensive, 1944; Citation, 1948; Ponder, 1949) plus Triple Crowns with Whirlaway and Citation.

Wright died in 1950, but his widow, Lucille, continued to operate Calumet at a very high level. Indeed, the farm added three more Kentucky Derbies to its stockpile in the '50s (Hill Gail in 1952; Iron Liege, 1957; and Tim Tam, 1958) and eventually garnered an eighth in 1968 (Forward Pass), although Calumet's racing fortunes had waned significantly by that time.

By 1977, though, when Alydar joined the Calumet racing stable, there were signs of a revival.

With an infusion of new talent from the farm, young trainer John

**Steve Cauthen lets out a victory whoop after the Derby**

Veitch had things going in the right direction by the time the strapping Alydar was ready to run in late spring. A powerfully built son of — ironically — Raise a Native, Alydar was out of the On-and-On mare Sweet Tooth, herself a product of one of Calumet's most productive female families, one noted for producing high-class stakes horses.

Veitch recalled that he realized from Alydar's first days in training the colt was a quick learner, "the star of the class" among Calumet's young horses. Alydar, in fact, demonstrated so much ability in morning workouts that Veitch had a tough time finding a maiden race whose entries would fill with him in the field, so he sent the colt postward for the first time in the Youthful Stakes at Belmont Park. In the five and a half-furlong race, the first-timer ran greenly to finish fifth behind the winner, a second-timer named Affirmed. No one watching that day could imagine what was about to happen between these two horses over the next fourteen months.

Affirmed, along with the other Harbor View horses, was getting his first racetrack lessons from the masterful Cuban-born trainer Laz Barrera, who had first gained national stature when he molded the fleet Bold Forbes into the 1976 Kentucky Derby and Belmont Stakes winner.

Bold Forbes had been essentially a miler whom Barrera had turned into a classic horse through shrewd and patient handling, but Affirmed demonstrated to Barrera and anyone else paying attention during the colt's juvenile year that he was much more than simply raw speed.

Winner of his first start, a maiden race, Affirmed then garnered his first stakes win in the aforementioned Youthful at the expense of the debuting Alydar, among others. The latter turned the tables on Affirmed in the Great American Stakes, after which the Harbor View colt won four straight, two of them major stakes victories (the Hopeful at Saratoga and the Belmont Futurity) over Alydar.

Alydar, too, had won four successive races following his career opening loss, including the Great American victory over Affirmed, prior to his head-to-head dustups with Affirmed. Alydar then beat Affirmed by a length and a quarter in the Champagne Stakes at Belmont but dropped a neck decision to his nemesis in the Laurel

Futurity. Veitch decided to run Alydar one more time, in the Remsen Stakes at Aqueduct, and caught a sloppy track and a sharp rival in Believe It, who won by two lengths.

Veitch felt his decision to run in the Remsen cost Alydar the two-year-old male title, but, more likely, Affirmed's 4-2 edge in head-on meetings swayed the voters. Affirmed ended the year with seven wins in nine starts, his only losses being to his Calumet rival, who wound up his own juvenile season with five wins in ten starts and runner-up honors in the polling for champion two-year-old male.

One thing was clear: The two were very closely matched, with three of their battles being settled by a half-length or less.

In the Experimental Free Handicap, the theoretical evaluation of the year's leading juveniles, Affirmed was assigned 126 pounds, one more than Alydar, two above Believe It.

Commentators and horsemen who had seen both were divided in their opinions as to which colt would be the better three-year-old. Some liked Affirmed's handiness and resolute character; others thought Alydar the more imposing physical specimen with more potential for improvement.

Whatever one's preference, one more thing was certain: both were exceptional talents who, with good health and a bit of luck, could make the 1978 "road to the Kentucky Derby" a memorable trip.

Affirmed's and Alydar's paths to the Kentucky Derby took different directions. Laz Barrera headed Affirmed to California, back to the state where the trainer had launched his own American career when he moved north from Mexico. He had made the same choice with Bold Forbes in 1976, in part because Barrera felt the mild winter weather was more congenial for daily training activities. However, Bold Forbes' races in California had not quite been what Barrera was looking for, so he shipped the colt to New York, where the trainer had prepared the three-year-old's way to the Churchill Downs winner's circle. The plan was to run Affirmed in the major California Triple Crown prep races, most notably the Santa Anita Derby.

Alydar, on the other hand, was off to Florida, the traditional base for the Calumet horses in the winter, especially with Lucille Markey and her husband, Admiral Gene Markey, in ill health and living in Miami for lengthy periods. Veitch had aim on the Flamingo Stakes at Hialeah and the Florida Derby at Gulfstream Park, with the Blue Grass Stakes at Keeneland as a likely final tune-up for the Derby.

ANNE M. EBERHARDT

**Laz Barrera**

Joining Alydar in Florida was his Remsen Stakes conqueror Believe It, a small son of In Reality trained by the redoubtable Woody Stephens for the Hickory Tree Stable of James Mills. Believe It's late fall wins in the Remsen and Keystone Race Track's Heritage Stakes gained him the third-place slot in the Experimental and made him a horse to contend with if either or both of his more notable competitors slipped.

Veitch gave Alydar a short breather at the end of the 1977 campaign but then slowly and steadily tightened the screws on the imposing and ever-growing Raise a Native colt. Alydar's first start of '78, a seven-furlong allowance race at Hialeah, where he trained, was nothing more than a fast walk in the sun in preparation for the Flamingo. Believe It also won handily over the same distance, setting up a Remsen rematch at Hialeah.

Meanwhile, Affirmed enjoyed something of an unintended holiday at Santa Anita, albeit not one endorsed by his trainer. The 1978 winter brought one of those occasional monsoon seasons that occur in southern California, and Santa Anita was mostly wet and muddy in January and February. Barrera never really considered shifting his training base eastward, although there was some thought that Affirmed might eventually race in New York on his way to Kentucky if his preparations in California were seriously compromised.

Affirmed spent many days walking the shed row of Barrera's barn

instead of going to the track, but he got in enough serious work to sprint a fast six and a half furlongs in winning an allowance race on March 8. Ten days later he sailed home on top in the mile and one-sixteenth San Felipe Handicap after being reminded of his mission several times by the whip of his jockey, eighteen-year-old riding sensation Steve Cauthen.

Affirmed wasn't in danger of losing the San Felipe; he simply liked to enjoy the view while traveling in front, doing what Cauthen referred to as "that little thing he likes to do with his ears," flicking them as he listened to the crowd noise, the chirp of low-flying birds, or the labored breathing of his would-be pursuers. Barrera and Cauthen both knew that days would come when such loafing would be problematic, so they wanted to keep Affirmed's head in the game, hence Cauthen's "love taps."

On April 2, in the Santa Anita Derby, the scenario was the same, with Affirmed leading all the way to tally an eight-length win after significant encouragement from jockey Laffit Pincay Jr., who replaced a

**Patrice and Louis Wolfson**

SANTA ANITA

**Affirmed easily wins the Santa Anita Derby as he preps for the Kentucky Derby**

suspended Cauthen for one race. (Cauthen had been a bit more aggressive in a race than the California stewards believed appropriate earlier in the Santa Anita meeting, so they grounded him for five days.)

After the Santa Anita Derby a few critics questioned Affirmed's attitude, wondering if the Kentucky Derby hopeful was getting too clever for his own good or perhaps even losing his competitive edge. Barrera called those ideas nonsense, saying his colt was fit both physically and mentally and would prove it in Kentucky. He believed Affirmed's relaxed style once the colt took command of a race was due to not having a horse capable of extending him.

Affirmed made one other stop along the western branch of the Derby trail. He journeyed across town for the April 16 Hollywood Derby at Hollywood Park, in lieu of a trip to New York for the Wood Memorial, an option Barrera eschewed because it meant two long trips — one to New York, another to Kentucky — to face horses Affirmed had already beaten. In the Hollywood Derby, as odds-on favorite, Affirmed put away the very fast Radar Ahead after six furlongs in 1:09 2/5, then, with the usual urging from Cauthen through the stretch, came to the wire two lengths in front of Think Snow.

Meanwhile, Alydar was leaving no doubt as to who was at the head of the pack marching toward Kentucky, at least on the eastern road. Already an impressive specimen at two, he was a larger, stronger, and more finished product by March of his sophomore season; and he ran to his looks in the Flamingo. After stalking the pace, the Calumet star surged past the leaders in early stretch and pulled away to a four and a half-length win in 1:47 for nine furlongs, a fast clocking even on a glib Hialeah surface.

Feeling that Alydar was on schedule for the tough races ahead, Veitch kept him in the barn for the Fountain of Youth Stakes, Gulfstream's main prep for the Florida Derby, which saw Sensitive Prince, a lightly raced, unbeaten son of 1969 Kentucky Derby winner Majestic Prince (yet another son of Raise a Native), edge Believe It.

Sensitive Prince stayed in his stall for the Florida Derby, but Believe It was back for more and challenged Alydar for the lead as the two turned for the stretch run. The Calumet ace responded to a pair of right-handed reminders from jockey Jorge Velasquez by drawing away to a two-length final margin, again traveling a mile and one-eighth in 1:47.

Next for Alydar was a trip home to Kentucky, where he would bed down at Keeneland in preparation for the Blue Grass Stakes on April 27. Keeneland, only a two-minute gallop from Alydar's birthplace at Calumet, would give him a chance to acclimate to Kentucky spring weather while gearing up for the upcoming rumble at Churchill Downs.

Elsewhere, other Derby prospects emerged, even if their chances to threaten the two big hitters were debatable.

A strong galloper with the clever name of Esops Foibles, a son of 1955 Horse of the Year Nashua, won both the Louisiana and Arkansas Derbies; and while his form didn't remind many of his sire, the promising three-year-old was bred to like the Kentucky Derby's mile and a quarter distance, something not a certainty for most Derby pretenders.

Farther north and east, just when some observers began to write him off, Believe It made a smashing mid-race move to win the Wood

Memorial by three and a half lengths over Darby Creek Road, an improving son of Roberto owned by John W. Phillips. Phillips was the son-in-law of Darby Dan Farm owner John W. Galbreath, who had won the 1963 and '67 Kentucky Derbies in upsets with Chateaugay and Proud Clarion, respectively, and rarely sent a horse to Churchill unless it had a respectable chance. As for Believe It, while being free of Alydar's shadow undoubtedly improved the colt's prospects for getting his picture taken in the winner's circle, no one could discount his resilience and tenacity, nor the canny judgment of trainer Woody Stephens.

Back in Kentucky, Alydar went postward in the Blue Grass against a moderate group of eight three-year-olds that figured to get sweaty while watching Alydar have the race to himself. The day was, in fact, more a sentimental journey than a horse race. Alydar and his eight overmatched foes got away from the gate properly, and everyone finished in good order, the others well astern of Alydar, who won by thirteen lengths in 1:49 3/5 for the nine furlongs over a drying-out track listed as "good."

What made the day special for thousands of Keeneland racegoers

MILT TOBY

**Alydar cruises to victory in the Blue Grass Stakes**

**Affirmed gallops under the Twin Spires before the Derby**

was the sideshow that became the main event. Keeneland President Ted Bassett, a gentleman to the core, made certain that Admiral and Mrs. Markey were not only driven over to Keeneland, but also parked near the rail at the top of the homestretch. During the post parade jockey Velasquez took Alydar over to the fence where the frail Lucille Markey was standing, stopped the horse, and said, "Here's your baby, my lady."

The Markeys were able to cheer Alydar to his bloodless victory then Veitch took the trophy to their car before they were driven home to Calumet. There were tears aplenty and thunderous applause for both the owners and their horse, although a few watchers questioned the wisdom of opening up the pipes with a horse so clearly superior to his rivals. Perhaps an easier trip would have been in order, given the task that lay ahead, nine days later.

Affirmed, by then also in Kentucky, had his training camp set up at Churchill Downs, and horsemen who had not seen him since the previous fall in the East were impressed with his development into a bigger, stronger, more masculine version of the prior year's sleek racing machine. If Alydar was a battleship, Affirmed was now a heavy cruiser, as nimble and quick as ever, but with more substance and power.

Affirmed's copper coat glistened in the mornings as the Harbor View runner took to the track, his one long work a mile and one-eighth trip in the slop on the Saturday before the Derby, timed in a tepid 1:56 1/5. The leisurely pace of the workout had initially disconcerted Barrera, but on reflection he noted that Affirmed had finished well. The trainer was pleased with a final serious work the following Wednesday, when his charge zipped five furlongs in :59.

Veitch sent Alydar an easy half-mile in :50 flat on the Tuesday prior to the Derby, a work that privately caused concern. "I didn't like the way he went," Veitch would say later. "He didn't do anything wrong, but he gave me a cloud of doubt." The trainer had figured out that Alydar needed a short, sharp blowout a day or two before a race, and accordingly the colt went three furlongs in :37 2/5 on the Friday before the Derby, not bad and not remarkable.

Finally, the time had come. The prep races and workouts were history. An eleven-horse field assembled for the 104th Derby, and more than 131,000 souls gathered under Churchill's Twin Spires to watch two of the most highly regarded Derby contenders in memory match strides. In fact, it was a rare occasion when the three top-rated two-year-olds from the previous year would make it to the Derby, much less as the top-heavy favorites.

An interesting question, even if irrelevant to the outcome of the Derby, was the matter of who would go to the starting gate as the favorite.

Affirmed had done nothing wrong in 1978 and did have four wins in six tries against his great rival, even if the contests had been close. Even so, Alydar might have improved at three. Affirmed could certainly make the same claim with regard to improvement, and there was the air of quiet but serious confidence among the Harbor View colt's connections. They weren't cocky, just certain.

Alydar, of course, was the hometown boy who had made good. He

was a throwback to the dominant days of the Calumet dynasty, when trainer Ben Jones and his son Jimmy seemed to have a perpetual production line sending the next good one their way. Alydar, like Affirmed, had done everything well as a three-year-old. Indeed, he had run faster times in two of his three nine-furlong races than had Affirmed in his two such efforts, lending support to the Calumet runner's fervent followers who wanted to believe the bigger, stronger, faster three-year-old model Alydar was superior to Affirmed, even if only slightly.

Obviously, much sentiment was involved in wagering on this Derby, especially Calumet-driven sentiment, and as such, Alydar loaded into the gate as the 6-5 favorite, with Affirmed at 9-5. In an ordinary year either horse would have been an odds-on choice, but this was not an ordinary year. Believe It figured to be the third choice, based on his Wood performance and overall record, but the crowd had fallen in love with Sensitive Prince's six-for-six record and the reputation of his trainer, Allen Jerkens, as a man practically capable of turning water into

**Affirmed races to Derby victory**

wine, or at least a man able to beat glamour horses with dark horses.

Sensitive Prince had ability but not much experience, and his only win over proven horses was his narrow victory over Believe It in Florida while carrying eight fewer pounds. Nonetheless, it wouldn't be the Derby without a promising mystery horse, so the final flash of the odds board had Sensitive Prince at 4.50-1 and Believe It at 7.40-1.

For those in attendance, or watching the national telecast, it was almost as if one could hear an announcer saying, "And in this corner, wearing the black and pink of Harbor View Farm, is the reigning champion of his class, that lean, mean, fighting machine, Aaaaaafirmmmmmmmmmmmed.

"In the other corner, wearing the red and blue of Calumet Farm, is the big, brawny bad boy of Kentucky, the mighty Aaaaleeedarrrrrrrrrrrrrrr!"

A fantasy, certainly, but this Derby had the distinct feel of one of those occasional heavyweight boxing matches that capture international attention, with all the hype and hoopla but without the bellicose behavior on the part of the principals.

The speed in the race figured to be 117-1 shot Raymond Earl, with Sensitive Prince nearby, and so the race unfolded, at least for a while. Jerkens' greatest fear was that Sensitive Prince would get too excited, another way of saying he wouldn't rate, and the veteran trainer was, unfortunately for his colt's hopes, correct.

Sensitive Prince grabbed the bit and jockey Mickey Solomone and roared by Raymond Earl as they clicked off the first quarter-mile in :22 3/5, the half in :45 3/5, great fractions for a sprint race or the Indy 500, frightening for Thoroughbreds trying to run a mile and a quarter for the first time in their lives.

Affirmed, slightly startled when Sensitive Prince rushed to the lead, was in about as happy a place as Cauthen and Barrera could want him, sitting in third place about five lengths behind the drag racers in front, waiting for the logical moment to turn his Formula One motor to the task of getting the roses.

Behind him, well behind, a surprise was taking place, and a not very pleasant one, if you were an Alydar fan. Breaking evenly from post position ten, the favorite dropped back steadily behind the hard-charging leaders, falling seventeen lengths off the pace and looking like a horse that would take no prominent part in the final outcome.

Velasquez would say after the race that the colt "seemed kind of uncomfortable, and I had to keep working to try to get him running ... It was as if he had no running on his mind."

Cauthen, after keeping an eye out for an Alydar who failed to materialize, prepared to ask Affirmed to run his race. As they moved past the tiring leaders on the final turn, Affirmed seemed poised to head for the winner's circle without further pressure; but rider Eddie Maple had Believe It in motion to Affirmed's outside as they swung into the homestretch, and the game Hickory Tree colorbearer got his head in front after a mile in 1:35 4/5.

Cauthen felt his mount quicken on his own to go with Believe It, but the young rider had not really asked Affirmed for his best, still harboring the notion that Alydar might be looming. Passing the quarter pole and straightening out for the stretch drive, Cauthen forgot Alydar and sent his horse forward, tapping him routinely with his stick to remind the ear-flicking Affirmed that the 104th Derby was a full mile and a quarter.

Alydar finally, ponderously, had begun to limber up, running past tired horses, then gathering momentum through the stretch in a manner that excited his fans momentarily. He rushed by Darby Creek Road with his sweeping stride, then overhauled the hard-trying Believe It in the final hundred yards, brushing him as he went by. Alydar made up two and a half lengths on Affirmed in the final eighth of a mile, but it was a case of much too little, much too late.

In front, Affirmed and Cauthen, masters of their universe, put the finishing touches on a work of art. Affirmed, ridden with authority until the issue was resolved, crossed the finish line a length and a half to the good, stopping the teletimer in an excellent 2:01 1/5. Alydar's late charge earned him second money by one and a quarter lengths over the hard-working Believe It, with Darby Creek Road four and a

### Kentucky Derby
### Purse: $125,000 Added

**8th Race  Churchill Downs - May 6, 1978. 104th running Kentucky Derby.**
Purse $125,000 added. Three-year-olds. 1 1-4 Miles. Main Track. Track: Fast.
Value of race $239,400. Net value to winner, $186,900 and gold trophy; second, $30,000; third, $15,000; fourth, $7,500.

| Horse | A | Wgt | Eqp | Odds | PP | 1/4 | 1/2 | 3/4 | 1 | Str | Fin | Jockey |
|---|---|---|---|---|---|---|---|---|---|---|---|---|
| Affirmed | 3 | 126 | | 1.80 | 2 | 2$^h$ | 3$^{2\frac{1}{2}}$ | 3$^{1\frac{1}{2}}$ | 2$^3$ | 1$^2$ | 1$^{1\frac{1}{2}}$ | S Cauthen |
| Alydar | 3 | 126 | b | 1.20 | 10 | 9$^h$ | 9$^5$ | 8$^h$ | 4$^h$ | 3$^3$ | 2$^{1\frac{1}{2}}$ | J Velasquez |
| Believe It | 3 | 126 | | 7.40 | 9 | 4$^{\frac{1}{2}}$ | 4$^{\frac{1}{2}}$ | 5$^3$ | 1$^h$ | 2$^2$ | 3$^{4\frac{1}{2}}$ | E Maple |
| Darby Creek Road | 3 | 126 | b | 33.00 | 7 | 7$^{\frac{1}{2}}$ | 7$^2$ | 7$^2$ | 5$^{\frac{1}{2}}$ | 4$^2$ | 4$^{2\frac{1}{2}}$ | D Brumfield |
| Esops Foibles | 3 | 126 | b | 49.70 | 3 | 5$^{1\frac{1}{2}}$ | 5$^4$ | 4$^1$ | 6$^3$ | 5$^3$ | 5$^{5\frac{1}{2}}$ | C J McCarron |
| Sensitive Prince | 3 | 126 | | 4.50 | 11 | 3$^{2\frac{1}{2}}$ | 1$^{1\frac{1}{2}}$ | 1$^3$ | 3$^{1\frac{1}{2}}$ | 6$^3$ | 6$^{\frac{1}{2}}$ | M Solomone |
| Dr. Valeri | 3 | 126 | b | 96.10 | 8 | 11 | 11 | 10$^4$ | 10$^5$ | 7$^{1\frac{1}{2}}$ | 7$^{3\frac{1}{2}}$ | R Riera Jr |
| Hoist the Silver | 3 | 126 | | 123.70 | 5 | 8$^2$ | 8$^{\frac{1}{2}}$ | 9$^5$ | 7$^3$ | 8$^5$ | 8$^7$ | R Depass |
| Chief of Dixieland | 3 | 126 | b | 121.70 | 6 | 6$^3$ | 6$^2$ | 6$^{\frac{1}{2}}$ | 9$^1$ | 9$^1$ | 9$^1$ | A Rini |
| Raymond Earl | 3 | 126 | | 117.10 | 1 | 1$^2$ | 2$^4$ | 2$^2$ | 8$^1$ | 10$^2$ | 10$^2$ | R L Baird |
| Special Honor | 3 | 126 | b | 177.10 | 4 | 10$^3$ | 10$^{\frac{1}{2}}$ | 11 | 11 | 11 | 11 | P Nicolo |

**Off Time:** 5:41    **Time Of Race:** :22$\frac{1}{2}$    :45$\frac{1}{2}$    1:10$\frac{1}{2}$    1:35$\frac{1}{2}$    2:01$\frac{1}{2}$
**Start:** Good For All but Special Honor    **Track:** Fast
**Equipment:** b for blinkers

**Mutuel Payoffs**

| 2 | Affirmed | $5.60 | $2.80 | $2.60 |
|---|---|---|---|---|
| 10 | Alydar | | 2.60 | 2.40 |
| 9 | Believe It | | | 2.80 |

**Winner:** Affirmed, ch. c. by Exclusive Native—Won't Tell You, by Crafty Admiral (Trained by Lazaro S. Barrera).
Bred by Harbor View Farm in Fla.

**Start good for all but Special Honor. Won driving.**
AFFIRMED away alertly but held in reserve for six furlongs, moved up boldly along outside thereafter to take command on second turn, relinquished the lead momentarily a quarter-mile out but responded to a rousing ride to regain command in upper stretch and was fully extended to hold ALYDAR safe. The latter, under snug restraint early, commenced to advance from the outside after six furlongs, continued wide into the stretch, swerved in to bump with BELIEVE IT in closing sixteenth and finished strongly when straightened. BELIEVE IT reserved off the early pace, moved up with a bold rush while bearing out on the second turn to gain command momentarily a quarter-mile away, continued wide while lacking a further response and was bumped by ALYDAR in the closing stages. DARBY CREEK ROAD lacked speed and hung after making a rally on the final bend. ESOPS FOIBLES faltered after making a mild bid on the second turn. SENSITIVE PRINCE sent to the fore on rounding the first turn, continued to make a swift pace while along the inside to final bend where he gave way suddenly. DR. VALERI was without speed. CHIEF OF DIXIELAND was bumped about before going a quarter-mile. RAYMOND EARL showed brief early speed and tired badly. SPECIAL HONOR reared at the start.

**Owners:** (1) Harbor View Farm; (2) Calumet Farm; (3) Hickory Tree Stable; (4) J W Phillips; (5) J Frankel; (6) Top of the Marc Stable; (7) V & R Renzi; (8) Dasso-Golob-Levinson-Solomon; (9) Dixie Jake Inc; (10) R N Lehmann; (11) Linda T Gaston & A D Haynes
©EQUIBASE

quarter lengths farther back in fourth.

Affirmed was officially "king of the ring," having achieved at least a technical knockout of his arch-rival.

Lou Wolfson, as proud as he could be of his homebred colt, was a gracious winner, saying that he could understand Alydar's favoritism, given the place Calumet held in racing history. Wolfson had earlier made discreet inquiries about buying Alydar and had great respect for the Calumet runner's talent and competitive spirit.

Veitch, likewise, was gracious in defeat, congratulating the winners and saying that he was "disappointed for the Markeys." Privately, he thought his colt, for whatever reason, did not really extend himself over the Churchill surface and had never gotten in a blow at Affirmed. He believed that the result in the next bouts — the Preakness and/or Belmont Stakes — would be more favorable for his charge.

Barrera, though, had a different idea, saying after the race: "They go one mile, they go five miles, it make no difference. Affirmed is just waiting for a horse that can make him run."

The 104th Derby was officially history, and excellent history it was. For the first time ever, the top three two-year-olds of the previous year had run one-two-three in the Derby.

Those watching suspected they'd seen something exceptional, a feat that was remarkable in itself given that the '70s was already the decade of Secretariat and Seattle Slew, Derby winners of legend.

That judgment would be resoundingly validated in the weeks and months ahead, as Affirmed and Alydar finished ever closer to each other in the successive Triple Crown races, coming to the wire as a team in the Belmont. Yet, each time Affirmed had the edge, even if only by the narrowest of margins.

Their final meeting took place in Saratoga's Travers Stakes, when Affirmed finished in front but was disqualified for fouling a surging Alydar as the field swept into the final turn. Although merited, the disqualification left an unsatisfactory end to horse racing's best-ever rivalry.

That huge crowd assembled at Churchill Downs on May 6, 1978, to see two great racehorses renew their head-to-head competition will never forget the two minutes, one and one-fifth seconds to which they were treated.

There have been faster Derbies, closer Derbies, more controversial Derbies, but no Derby with two more talented or courageous performers on display, a race for the ages between two horses for the ages.

The first Saturday in May will never be better.

*By Timothy T. Capps*

# Money in the Bank
## (Citation, 1948)

THE SEEDS OF GREATNESS are sometimes sown in loss. Calumet Farm's owner Warren Wright watched the 1938 Kentucky Derby with complete and utter disappointment as his Bull Lea, the $2.90-1 second choice in the ten-horse field, never got on track and finished a dismal eighth.

The winner, Woolford Farm's Lawrin, bounded away in the stretch under the Twin Spires of Churchill Downs with twenty-two-year-old jockey Eddie Arcaro. Wright, never one to take failure well, had seen enough. Impressed by Lawrin's trainer, Benjamin Allyn "Plain Ben" Jones, Wright soon hired him. The alliance, which also included Jones' son Jimmy, would produce a battalion of major stakes winners that would take Thoroughbred racing by storm.

Through a twist of fate, the Jones boys, in the spring of 1948, would team Arcaro with a strapping dark bay son from the fifth crop of Bull Lea to form a partnership that would transcend not only the Kentucky Derby but also the Triple Crown to deliver one of horse racing's most memorable seasons.

Citation, who by the time he captured the Derby drew comparisons to the legendary Man o' War, would become a racing icon — an iron horse in a golden era in American Thoroughbred history. No other horse would even come close to being uttered in the same breath until Secretariat took the sporting world by storm twenty-five years later in the spring and summer of 1973.

Through four racing seasons Citation won thirty-two of forty-five starts, finishing second ten times and third twice. Citation ran off the board only once, finishing fifth in a race in the twilight of his career. He put together a five-race and then a seven-race winning streak, only to surpass them with a record sixteen consecutive wins, a feat that wasn't matched until nearly fifty years later. More important, during the post-war days of the 1940s, he became racing's first millionaire in an age where a hundred-thousand-dollar purse was a rarity, not a weekly occurrence.

Arcaro, a Hall of Fame jockey and rider of five Derby winners including Calumet Farm's Triple Crown winner Whirlaway, called Citation the best horse he had ever ridden. He told *The Blood-Horse* magazine years later that during the 1948 Belmont Stakes, "[Citation] was so fast he scared me."

Calumet Farm was already the gold standard of Thoroughbred operations by 1948, Citation's three-year-old year, but it hadn't started out that way. The farm traced its roots to 1910, when William Wright, Warren's father, built a farm near Libertyville, Illinois, with the goal of breeding top-class Standardbreds. A successful businessman who built the Calumet Baking Powder Company from a six-man operation in Chicago to a national brand, the senior Wright found a few golden nuggets in the trotting business as well. He purchased another farm, this one outside Lexington, Kentucky, to expand his operation. He had plenty of capital to work with, having sold his business for $30 million to Postum, a company later named General Foods.

However, the trotting business was not a moneymaker for the business-minded father-and-son team. Upon his father's death in 1931, ironically the same year the Wright-bred Calumet Butler won the Hambletonian, harness racing's most prestigious event, Warren Wright began turning the Kentucky farm into a Thoroughbred operation. Warren Wright struggled at first, but once he got the Jones boys in his employ, his fortunes quickly began to change.

Ben Jones had started training horses in his youth and won his first race as a trainer in Fort Worth, Texas. No up-and-comer when Lawrin won the Derby in 1938, Jones had sent out his first "recognized" winner, Errant Lady, at Oklahoma City in 1909.

Ben and Jimmy Jones began training the Calumet horses in September 1939. By the spring of 1941, they were in the Churchill Downs winner's circle with Whirlaway, who would go on to win the Triple Crown and take Calumet Farm to the top of the earnings standings.

THE BLOODHORSE

**A formidable trio: Citation, Eddie Arcaro, and Jimmy Jones**

Citation came into the world as Calumet Farm was establishing itself as a racing and breeding powerhouse. Foaled on April 11, 1945, Citation was the third foal out of the Hyperion mare Hydroplane II. From the beginning he showed promise, as did another son of Bull Lea — Coaltown, out of Easy Lass, by Blenheim II.

The Joneses usually ranked the coming year's crop of runners. According to then farm manager Paul Ebelhardt, Citation and Coaltown were at the head of the pack. The 1945 crop also included a precocious filly named Bewitch by Bull Lea out of the Wildair mare Potheen. As the group readied to head to Florida in November 1946, Ebelhardt said that Citation was "the perfect specimen of a Thoroughbred." Citation didn't have one particular outstanding attribute, the balance of his conformation being the key to his ideal physique.

While Calumet Farm, in the cradle of the Bluegrass, was an idyllic place to raise Thoroughbreds, Ben Jones attributed success more to the powerhouse breeding stock there, especially to the potency of Bull Lea. Prior to the 1948 Kentucky Derby, a *Daily Racing Form* reporter asked Jones about Calumet as the birthplace for so many great horses, and he responded, "Give me Bull Lea and 20 ranking broodmares, and I'll go most anywhere and produce you some horses which could run."

The Joneses had their training regime for their young horses down to a science, starting with taking the yearlings to Florida to be broken and turned into racehorses. The routine started with a little down time to get the youngsters acclimated and was followed with a long and steady introduction to learning their starting gate manners before they were actually asked to run. As the winter of 1946 turned to the spring of 1947, the Joneses split the stable, with Ben taking a string to the Keeneland meet at Kentucky and Jimmy taking the string that headed east.

Coaltown, whom many on the farm believed was the best of the lot, would not get a chance to strut his stuff at two. A throat disorder kept him sidelined until his three-year-old year. Citation, however, was itching to get his racing career under way.

Citation debuted in a four and a half-furlong maiden race at the old

THE COURIER-JOURNAL AND LOUISVILLE TIMES

**Warren Wright accepts the Derby trophy from Churchill's Matt Winn**

Havre de Grace track in Maryland on April 22 under rider Albert Snider. Over a track rated slow, Citation rallied from three lengths off the pace to win by a half-length in :54 2/5. He didn't exactly set the world on fire, but he showed determination along with a nice turn of foot, running the final eighth in :12 flat.

Citation's first race mildly impressed Jimmy Jones, but the colt's next two races captivated the trainer. On May 3 at Pimlico, Citation crushed an allowance field by three and a half lengths, finishing five furlongs in 1:01 1/5 in a wire-to-wire effort, again under Snider. Eighteen days later, back at Havre de Grace, the Calumet juvenile came from off the pace to win another five-furlong allowance by one and three-quarters lengths, getting the trip in a quick :59 1/5. Meanwhile at Keeneland, Bewitch was running a hole in the wind for Ben Jones. A pair of wins came in mid-April, and then on April 30 at Churchill Downs, Bewitch blew away her rivals by eight lengths in the Debutante Stakes, covering five furlongs in 1:00 3/5.

As the spring turned to summer, the best of Calumet's two-year-olds headed for Chicago. Citation made short work of an allowance field at

FINISH

MAY
1
RACE
7

It's all Citation at the finish as he hits the wire with ears pricked

Arlington Park on July 24 and then won the Elementary Stakes at Washington Park less than a week later, going six furlongs in 1:10 3/5.

What would happen there in mid-August is a lesson in the power of the Calumet stable of the 1940s.

The six-furlong, $78,000 Washington Futurity featured not one, not two, but three Calumet runners: Citation, Bewitch, and Free America. The Jones boys were convinced that they could sweep the rich race. After all, Bewitch was unbeaten in seven starts; Citation, unbeaten in five; and Free America was riding a three-race win streak after dropping his debut.

One trainer said that the only way to avoid Calumet was to "stay at home or ship to Winnipeg." By all means, trainers wanting to avoid the Calumet juggernaut should have left Illinois.

Jockey Doug Dodson, who had ridden Citation in the colt's two wins in Chicago, would ride Bewitch, who the Jones boys thought was invincible. Snider, serving a suspension, was unable to ride Citation, so the Joneses signed on Steve Brooks, who would ride Calumet's Ponder to victory in the 1949 Derby. Jackie Westrope, who would eventually find his way to the Hall of Fame, was to ride Free America.

Seven other entries showed up, but they were merely window dressing for the Calumet trio. Such was the power of this trio that the Jones boys were reported as saying that whoever was in front in the stretch should be allowed to win the whole thing. More than likely that would be Bewitch.

Bewitch, who had the most speed of the bunch, broke away from the pack, opening up a four-length lead. Citation sat in fourth, some four or five lengths from the lead. Free America bided his time at the back of the pack. Bewitch widened her lead turning for home and had six lengths on Citation at the eighth pole, but "Cy" began to pick up steam despite some "restraint" from the usually hard-riding Brooks. Free America closed on the outside. It wasn't until late that Brooks let out a notch and let Citation run. He finished second, a length behind Bewitch and a head in front of Free America. Calumet had run one-two-three, just as the Joneses predicted. To this day, there is plenty of

BERT CLARK THAYER

**Jimmy Jones (center) leads Citation (right) and a stablemate to the track**

speculation that the "fix" was in by letting Bewitch win.

It would be a long time before Citation would feel the sting of defeat again.

Three more races awaited Citation on the East Coast that fall, and the mighty one had little trouble with the first two at Belmont, salving his wounded pride with a victory in the Futurity Trial and then winning the rich Futurity itself, both sprints over the old Widener course at Belmont Park with Snider aboard. In the Trial, Citation broke ninth in the fourteen-horse field and still managed to win by a length, "drawing away." He was on the engine in the October 4 Futurity and cruised to a three-length win. Bewitch, coming off a tough effort in the Matron in which she had finished first but was disqualified to last, lost again in the Futurity, finishing third behind Citation and Whirling Fox.

The mile and one-sixteenth Pimlico Futurity on November 8 was the icing on the cake for Citation's exemplary season. Citation won by a length and a half under Dodson even though the colt was running two turns and testing a muddy track for the first time.

Calumet Farm and the Jones boys were convinced they had a champion, and they were right. Citation had eight wins from nine starts and earnings of $155,680, and he was the unanimous choice as champion two-year-old colt or gelding of *Daily Racing Form*. Joining Calumet's cavalcade of stars were two-year-old filly champ Bewitch and the older star Armed, who was named Horse of the Year.

The easy winter-book favorite for the 1948 Kentucky Derby, Citation was among a string of horses sent to Hialeah racetrack in Miami. Despite Citation's championship performance as a two-year-old, backstretch whispers indicated Calumet might have a "better one in the barn." Lurking in the shadows was Coaltown, who was gearing up to flash his own championship form.

Citation received little rest in Florida and made an unconventional three-year-old debut against older horses on Groundhog Day, February 2. At weight for age, Citation toted a mere 113 pounds, and Snider was back aboard. It was an easy win against six rivals, among which was Armed, who carried 130 pounds and finished sixth.

The win over older horses boosted Citation's stock even higher. The accolades came from every direction, even from legendary trainer Sunny Jim Fitzsimmons, who spoke volumes when he told reporters that "up to this point Citation's done more than any horse I ever saw — and I saw Man o' War."

The comparisons would continue.

Gearing up for the prestigious Kentucky Derby preps of the Everglades and Flamingo stakes, Citation again faced older horses in the seven-furlong Seminole Handicap at Hialeah. Under 112 pounds, he battled early but was able to pull away to win by a length.

Stretching out to nine furlongs, Citation had little trouble winning the Everglades on February 18 by a length and the Flamingo ten days later by six lengths. That was four telltale wins in the shortest month of the year.

At about the same time, Ben Jones unveiled the quietly anticipated

GULFSTREAM PHOTO SERVICE

**The Calumet-bred Coaltown would prove Citation's biggest challenge**

Coaltown. Proving to be the star the trainer thought, the colt broke his maiden by two and a half lengths on February 3 with Dodson aboard. Coming right back on February 26 with Snider aboard, Coaltown ran a record-equaling six furlongs in 1:09 3/5 against a field of ten other three-year-olds. Taking the lead from the start, Coaltown had a three-length lead after a half-mile in :45 2/5, then pulled away with ease to win by twelve lengths as the heavy favorite. The racing world was gearing up for a super spring, leading up to the Derby, when tragedy struck the Citation camp.

On March 5 Snider joined several horsemen on a yacht for a day of fishing off the Florida Keys. Three of the men, including Snider, took a skiff off the yacht to flat fish. A deadly electrical storm whipped up off the coast, and the threesome was lost. The skiff was recovered but none of the bodies, and the racing world mourned the loss.

It didn't take an expert to realize that Citation's new rider should be

Arcaro, who had proven himself to be the top jockey in the nation, having already won three Kentucky Derbies and piloted the Triple Crown-winning Whirlaway.

Off his strenuous February, Citation had been given March off, but Arcaro got to know him during morning workouts. While Citation rested, Coaltown's stock soared. Ben Jones then shipped Coaltown to Lexington and sent him against older horses in the Phoenix Hotel Handicap on April 8, a field that he dispensed with ease by two and a half lengths. Coaltown then broke the track record in the Blue Grass Stakes, getting the mile and one-eighth in 1:49 1/5 and setting the stage for a terrific showdown at Churchill Downs.

Citation, meanwhile, was shipped back to Maryland to prep for the Derby in the Chesapeake Stakes at Havre de Grace. In the April 12 Chesapeake Trial at six furlongs, Arcaro, in his first ride aboard Citation, made an egregious mistake that led to the colt's second defeat.

Citation, after a somewhat sluggish start, tracked the pace of a horse

**Citation wins the Everglades at Hialeah on his way to the Derby**

named Saggy over the muddy going. When the field turned for home, Arcaro attempted to go wide around Saggy and a horse named Hefty. Changing leads as he came out of the turn, Hefty bolted to the outside and carried Citation and Arcaro with him. As Arcaro regrouped to get by Hefty, Saggy, alone on the lead, went on to win by a length.

The loss and a critical press tarnished Citation's sterling reputation and embarrassed both Arcaro and Jimmy Jones. "Cy" rebounded to win the April 17 Chesapeake Stakes by an easy four and a half lengths before joining Coaltown in Kentucky for the Derby. Three previous Derby winners had used a victory in the Chesapeake to launch their bid for the roses, the last being Sam Riddle's War Admiral, a son of Man o' War, in 1937.

In somewhat of a surprise move, the Joneses entered Citation in the Derby Trial Stakes the Tuesday before the May 1 Run for the Roses. Despite Citation's solid win in the one-mile Trial over a fast track, racing historians were quick to note that no winner of the Trial had gone on to win the Derby. (Black Gold won the Derby Trial Purse, the precursor to the Trial, prior to winning the 1924 Derby.) Also, to that point, no winner of Belmont's Futurity had gone on to win the Derby the following year, so the Jones boys were out to burst a pair of Derby precedents.

Showing just how "iron" he was, Citation blew out three furlongs in :36 2/5 on the Thursday before the Derby, just two days after the Trial.

The night before the Derby, the Joneses met with Arcaro and Newbold Leroy Pierson, who would ride Coaltown. Arcaro, who still doubted whether he was on the "right" horse to win the Derby, later spoke with Ben Jones. The elder Jones, who had trained Coaltown longer, put the rider at ease, by telling him, "Eddie, you can sleep well tonight, because, and you can take this as gospel: Any horse Citation can see, he can catch. And he's got perfect eyesight."

Horsemen assembling in Louisville knew the Jones boys had the Derby surrounded, but they were split on which colt would wear the roses. "Calumet Farm's Citation and Coaltown appear to have this Kentucky Derby at their mercy," trainer Dan Stewart told the *Daily Racing Form*.

Usually trainers for the Derby fret over the competition, but in the Calumet camp they were fretting over which of their colts would win. Citation was the steady performer; Coaltown, the quicker, Johnny-come-lately challenger. Jimmy Jones was certain Citation was the better.

Jones would tell *The Blood-Horse* decades later: "When I come up to Louisville with Citation, some of them boys from Louisville started kidding me, sayin', 'What you doin' here?' I told them, 'I come over to win the Derby.' They said, 'You won't see anything but a big brown hiney (of Coaltown), that's all you'll see.' I said, 'If he beats this horse, you can call me imbecile for the rest of my life.'"

Jimmy Jones was no imbecile, but it would take a world-class performance under the Twin Spires of Churchill Downs to prove him right.

Jimmy, who had trained Citation, deferred to his father and let the horse run in Ben's name. Such was the strength of family ties. Another Derby victory by Ben Jones would put him among racing's elite trainers, tying him at four with H.J. "Derby Dick" Thompson for the most Derby wins.

While the connections of 109 three-year-olds had ponied up the fifty-dollar nomination fee back in February for the seventy-fourth running of the Kentucky Derby, only seven entered and only six made it to the starting gate.

C.A. O'Neil Jr.'s Galedo drew the rail but was scratched, putting Citation in post one and Coaltown in post two. From there out were Escadru, Grandpere, Billings, and My Request.

Horseplayers considered Citation invincible enough that the colt had created minus pools in his past three starts. Churchill Downs president Matt Winn so feared losing money on the track's signature race that he declared patrons could only place win money on the Derby with its double-dynamite entry of Citation and Coaltown, who faced just four other betting interests.

The 1948 Derby marked the first time in Derby pari-mutuel wagering that bettors could place only win wagers. The morning line on the duo was 1-5, the shortest in the race's history. The shortest previous odds were 1-4 on Himyar in the 1878 running.

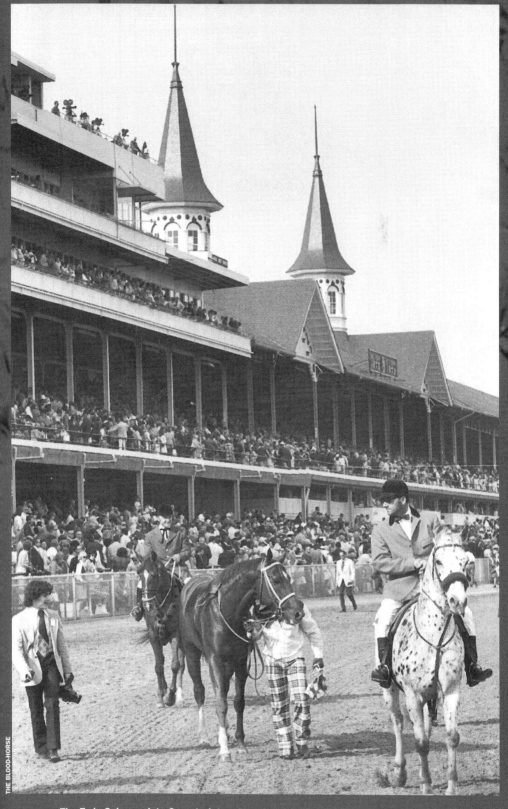

The Twin Spires salute Secretariat as he returns to the barn after his Derby triumph

A cool and collected Secretariat in the Derby post parade

Canonero II gallops out after his stunning Derby victory

Viva Venezuela! Canonero II's connections celebrate in the winner's circle

**Ben Jones (right) leads Citation to the winner's circle as Jimmy Jones (left) congratulates Eddie Arcaro**

In one of the closest Derby finishes ever, Iron Liege (inside) gets a nose in front of Gallant Man

As Affirmed (right) prepares to take the lead, Alydar (far left) begins moving up on the turn

Alysheba nearly goes to his knees in the stretch of the 1987 Derby but recovers to win

Ben F. Whitaker's My Request, unbeaten in four starts that season, was the Calumet entry's toughest competition in the Derby. Overall, the son of Requested—Sugapud, by Sickle, had won ten of seventeen starts with four placings. Trainer James Conway named Doug Dodson to ride. The colt had faced Citation once, running seventh behind him in the previous year's Futurity at Belmont under Eric Guerin.

For what would turn out to be one of the greatest Derbies of all time, the weather did not provide the ideal backdrop. At about 3:30 that morning it started raining — pouring, in fact. The track for the Derby would be "off." But that didn't stop the crowds from descending on Churchill Downs. As the rains abated near dawn, leaving mostly cloudy skies, growing clusters of fans assembled around the track, waiting for the gates to open. When all was said and done, approximately a hundred thousand people turned out to see if Calumet's pair was as good as advertised.

Arcaro only had two mounts on the card prior to the Derby, winning the second race astride Grand Barter in a five-furlong maiden sprint. Calumet Farm didn't have a starter other than its big two.

My Request opened as the 3-2 early favorite when the Derby odds first flashed on the toteboard that afternoon. The Calumet pair was 8-5. However, the money began flooding in on the entry, and by post time the stablemates were 2-5.

In the paddock before the race, the Jones boys were exuding confidence, with Jimmy exchanging small talk with Arcaro, and with Ben reminding Pierson of Coaltown's speed and penchant for being on the front end.

Pierson was instructed to grab the early lead on Coaltown and set the pace. But when the gates sprang open, Citation broke out ahead. Arcaro, though, quickly took back on Cy and let Coaltown and Pierson find their way to the front. Coaltown set about his business, flashing an opening quarter in :23 2/5 with Citation in second and My Request and Billings right on Cy's heels. As the short field rounded the first turn, Arcaro took Citation off the rail for a clear run, allowing room for his competitors on the inside. Up ahead Coaltown opened up a sizable six-length lead, getting the first half-mile of the mile and a quarter Derby in a brisk :46 3/5 over the sloppy track.

Citation remained in second, having just a head advantage over Grandpere. It was two lengths back to a tight bunch of My Request, Billings, and Escadru. Coaltown continued to roll down the back-stretch uncontested on the lead. Arcaro bided his time aboard Citation, knowing his horse would soon have to make a run at Coaltown, but Arcaro didn't panic. With five furlongs clicked off in :59 1/5 and with five furlongs remaining, Citation cut ever so slightly into Coaltown's lead, trimming it to three and a half lengths. Citation had his rival in his sights, but the others behind Citation were beginning to lose sight of him. As Coaltown rounded the far turn with Citation in pursuit, the rest of the field began to flag.

On the turn Arcaro cut Citation loose, and they quickly started gaining ground. The mile went in 1:38 as Citation eased up to Coaltown on the outside, getting right to his flank. The twin pair of devil's red-and-blue silks were in their own race — it was five lengths back to My Request, who was separating himself from Billings. Longshots Grandpere and Escadru were no longer in the contest.

Citation and Arcaro collared Coaltown and Pierson as they came out of the turn with three-sixteenths of a mile to go. Flying on the out-side, the two ran as a team for a while, but the stronger, more experi-enced Citation began to ease away. Citation hit the eighth pole in 1:51 2/5, holding a two-length lead over Coaltown. It was another four lengths back to My Request.

Citation pulled away, widening the distance between him and Coaltown with each powerful stride. Citation and Arcaro hit the wire three and a half lengths in front, getting the ten furlongs in 2:05 2/5. Coaltown continued driving to the wire, clearly the best of the others but still in the shadow of his more accomplished stablemate. Coaltown had three lengths on My Request at the line, with My Request topping Billings by one and a half lengths. Grandpere and Escadru were some twenty lengths back.

Wright headed to the winner's circle to greet his coveted third

THE BLOOD-HORSE

**Citation with Lucille Wright**

Derby winner, as did the Joneses. Arcaro took his record a notch higher, recording his fourth Derby win and later finding himself on the cover of the May 17 issue of *Time* magazine.

The great Turf writer Charles Hatton wrote after the Kentucky Derby: "Perhaps there have been more impressive Derby winners, but we do not recall one in 30 years of watching the race. Citation actually outbroke Coaltown, then spotted him seven lengths. It seemed impossible any colt could thus 'defy the lightning,' but Citation caught him with a tremendous run around the last turn and won pricking his ears.

"Ben Jones opines that a really worthwhile prospect ought to have at least one extremely fast furlong in his repertoire. 'Citation can uncork one most any time in his races,' he added.

"Such versatility is rarely wrapped up in the same horse hide, and this seems to us to be the remarkable thing about the 1948 Kentucky Derby winner."

Hatton, who popularized the term "Triple Crown," knew racing, especially when it came to three year olds.

The earlier comparisons to the great Man o' War rang with more truth now. Man o' War, once beaten by Upset as a two-year-old when the legendary chestnut broke badly going six furlongs at Saratoga, didn't even debut as a three-year-old until the Preakness Stakes, and here was another horse of similar caliber. Citation had won fifteen of seventeen starts — with a loss to stablemate Bewitch and then the loss to Saggy in the slop at Havre de Grace as his only "true" defeat.

An editorial in *The Blood-Horse* stated, "Citation stands in about the same position of complete domination as did Man o' War after the Preakness Stakes of 1920."

About the only people worrying about the Calumet juggernaut were track operators who feared paying out minus pools on Citation and Coaltown in the future. Luckily for them, with Citation being the only one capable of winning the Triple Crown, Coaltown was taken out of consideration for the Preakness.

After such a dominating performance, few wanted to take on the mighty Citation, and only three other horses lined up against Citation at Pimlico for the Preakness in Baltimore. So powerful was his reputation, that Citation went postward at odds of 1-10 — the eleventh consecutive time he had been odds-on.

Again, the weather didn't cooperate, with rains rendering the track "heavy" the afternoon of May 15. Citation broke from the outside four post, took the lead from the onset, and dictated the tempo while under "stout" restraint by Arcaro. The favorite set sensible fractions of :24 4/5 and :50 2/5. Citation had a length and a half advantage over 30-1 shot

Vulcan's Forge, and the race at that point was as good as over. Citation's lead widened to two lengths, then three lengths as he galloped alone on the front. With two cracks of the whip from Arcaro, Citation increased his lead in the stretch at Old Hilltop, hitting the wire five and a half lengths in front of Vulcan's Forge. Bovard, the 9-1 second choice was third, with Better Self finishing last. The time for the mile and three-sixteenths was a slow 2:02 2/5, but given the track condition and lack of competition, time was irrelevant considering the ease of his win.

To become the eighth winner of the Triple Crown, Citation had one race to go. However, with four weeks to the Belmont Stakes, the Joneses did not permit Citation to rest on his laurels. On May 29 Citation went after the mile and a quarter Jersey Stakes, with a rich $50,000-added purse. Only four colts took him on, and again after taking the lead at the break, Citation toyed with his rivals and pulled away to an eleven-length victory. His time of 2:03 set a track record at the old Garden State Park.

The stage was set for Citation to take New York by storm on June 12. Seven others were brave enough to pass the entry box, with Escadru taking some action as the 6-1 second choice. King Ranch's Better Self, coupled with Gasparilla, was 12-1.

If there was one nagging question, it was Citation's pedigree. With the sprint-slanted Bull Lea as his sire, Citation faced the Belmont challenge of twelve furlongs as the only remaining straw in his path. The distance would prove not to matter one whit.

With a twinge of tenseness in the air and a fast track for the first time in the Triple Crown series, Citation and Arcaro stumbled at the break while starting from the rail, but they quickly recovered and found the lead. Pressed by longshot Faraway, Citation set splits of :24 and :48 2/5 as they rounded the turn. The rest of the field seemed tentative, as if waiting for Arcaro and Citation to make a mistake. They didn't.

The lead began to widen as they passed the mile marker in 1:37, and Citation shook off Faraway like a fly on his shoulder. Coming out of the turn, Arcaro shook Citation up a bit, as if to tell him this was the real deal, and the lead quickly grew to four lengths, the mile and a quarter going in 2:02 3/5. The Belmont crowd roared as Escadru began to tire of trying to catch greatness.

Citation won the Belmont by eight lengths over Better Self, getting the demanding mile and a half in an easy 2:28 1/5, just three-fifths of a second off Bolingbroke's record set in 1942. Escadru was a half-length back in third, followed by Vulcan's Forge, who the week before had upset Coaltown in the one-mile Withers Stakes.

Although Citation became the fourth Triple Crown winner of the decade, he stood apart from predecessors Whirlaway, Count Fleet, and Assault with his complete dominance of the division and his fearlessness against older horses in his first sophomore races.

For Wright and the Jones boys Citation had more worlds to conquer. Citation would make nine more starts as a three-year-old and win them all — a distinction that would place him among the greatest of all time.

Seventeen wins in eighteen starts for the year … what could be next? Citation's accomplishments perhaps should have required no encore, but Jimmy Jones sent the colt to California, where he bagged an allowance at Tanforan, then won the Tanforan Handicap on December 11 by five lengths. However, the iron horse came out of the race with a sore left foreleg. Citation was diagnosed with an osselet, a stress injury that causes the fetlock joint to swell, calcify, and then gather more fluid. Jones wanted to give the colt some time at the farm. Wright disagreed and ordered Citation sent to Florida with the rest of the stable. Citation remained in training, but the injury suffered at the end of his three-year-old campaign kept him from the races for the entire 1949 season. Still, he could rest on his laurels. The accolades he gathered for 1948 were aplenty: Horse of the Year, champion handicap horse, and champion three-year-old.

Making his way back at five, his win streak briefly continued in an allowance race at Santa Anita on January 11, 1950, but came to an end at sixteen in a six thousand-dollar handicap on January 26. The old boy had lost more than a step in his time off, and the losses began to mount.

### Kentucky Derby
### Purse: $100,000 Added

**7th Race  Churchill Downs - May 1, 1948. Seventy-fourth running Kentucky Derby.**
**Purse $100,000 added. Three-year-olds. 1 1-4 Miles. Main Track. Track: Sloppy.**
**Gross Value, $111,450. Net value to winner, $83,400 and gold trophy; second, $10,000; third, $5,000; fourth, $2,500. Mutuel pool, $670, 833.**

| Horse | A | Wgt | Eqp | Odds | PP | ST | 1/2 | 3/4 | 1 | Str | Fin | Jockey |
|-------|---|-----|-----|------|----|----|-----|-----|---|-----|-----|--------|
| Citation | 3 | 126 | w | a-.40 | 1 | 2 | 2$^h$ | 2$^3$ | 2$^5$ | 1$^2$ | 1$^{3/4}$ | E Arcaro |
| Coaltown | 3 | 126 | wb | a-.40 | 2 | 1 | 1$^6$ | 1$^{3/4}$ | 1$^x$ | 2$^4$ | 2$^3$ | N L Pierson |
| My Request | 3 | 126 | w | 3.80 | 6 | 3 | 4$^h$ | 4$^3$ | 3$^{1/2}$ | 3$^1$ | 3$^{1/4}$ | D Dodson |
| Billings | 3 | 126 | w | 14.70 | 5 | 6 | 5$^x$ | 3$^x$ | 4$^8$ | 4$^{15}$ | 4$^{20}$ | M Peterson |
| Grandpere | 3 | 126 | w | 17.80 | 4 | 4 | 3$^2$ | 6 | 6 | 5$^x$ | 5$^{nk}$ | J Gilbert |
| Escadru | 3 | 126 | wb | 7.10 | 3 | 5 | 6 | 5$^6$ | 5$^{1/2}$ | 6 | 6 | A Kirkland |

a-Coupled, Citation and Coaltown.

**Off Time:** 4:33    **Time Of Race:** :23$^{2/5}$    :46$^{1/5}$    1:11$^{2/5}$    1:38    2:05$^{2/5}$
**Start:** Good For All    **Track:** Sloppy
**Equipment:** w for whip; b for blinkers

**Mutuel Payoffs**
| 1 | Calumet Farm entry | $2.80 |
|---|---|---|

NO PLACE OR SHOW MUTUELS SOLD.

**Winner:**  Citation, b. c. by Bull Lea—Hydroplane II, by Hyperion (Trained by B. A. Jones).
Bred by Calumet Farm in Ky.

**Start good from stall gate. Won handily; second and third driving.**
CITATION, away forwardly and losing ground while racing back of COALTOWN to the stretch, responded readily to a steady hand ride after disposing of the latter and drew clear. COALTOWN began fast, established a clear lead before going a quarter and, making the pace on the inside in the stretch, continued willingly, but was not good enough for CITATION, although easily best of the others. MY REQUEST, bothered slightly after the start, was in hand while improving his position to the stretch, then failed to rally when set down for the drive. BILLINGS suffered interference after the break when GRANDPERE bore to the outside, was in close quarters on the first turn when caught between ESCADRU and CITATION, then could not better his position when clear. GRANDPERE broke into BILLINGS at the start, displayed speed for a half-mile, then gave way. ESCADRU, forced to take up when in close quarters entering the backstretch, could not reach serious contention thereafter and tired badly after going three-quarters of a mile.
Scratched—Galedo, 126.

**Owners:**  (1) Calumet Farm; (2) Calumet Farm; (3) B F Whitaker; (4) Walmac Stable; (5) Mrs J P Adams; (6) W L Brann
©EQUIBASE

He lost to British import Noor in four monumental efforts — all record-breaking performances. His nose loss to Noor in the San Juan Capistrano Handicap would be the "greatest race" Jimmy Jones said he ever saw.

Citation was pressed on in pursuit of becoming racing's first millionaire; a then ill Wright still longed for his star to be more than the one-of-a-kind horse he already was. Wright died December 12, 1950, while Citation was the all-time money earner but remained short of seven figures. Citation finally got to $1,085,760 with a win in the Hollywood Gold Cup on July 14, 1951.

Retired to stud, Citation was a good but not great sire. From his first crop, Calumet Farm's Fabius ran second in the 1956 Kentucky Derby and then won the Preakness, but subsequent foals, except for champion three-year-old filly Silver Spoon, didn't have the same star power. Citation lived to the ripe old age of twenty-five, dying on August 8, 1970.

His achievements were monumental among mere mortals. He was a Triple Crown winner and racing's first millionaire; and upon him had been bestowed an embarrassment of riches in championship titles, as well as enshrinement in the Hall of Fame when its charter class was inducted in 1959.

Few before and even fewer after were of his caliber. His sixteen-race win streak was matched by Cigar during the 1994–96 seasons but never bettered. Of *The Blood-Horse*'s top one hundred Thoroughbreds of the twentieth century, Citation ranked third, behind only Man o' War and Secretariat — the three always mentioned in the same breath in a discussion of racing's upper crust.

His Kentucky Derby was the peak on the bell curve of the most famous streak in racing's grand history — facing one of the stiffest tests of his lengthy career when he ran down the loose-on-the-lead Coaltown in the mud under the Twin Spires. Citation's legendary performance in the spring of 1948 has ever strengthened the lore, and the allure, of the Kentucky Derby.

*By Evan I. Hammonds*

# The Fighting Finish
## (Brokers Tip, 1933)

THE GREAT DEPRESSION hit the country hard, and Thoroughbred racing suffered along with the rest of America. Many fans no longer had the energy or wherewithal to follow the horses. As the 1933 Derby field came together, no particular horses stood out, and it seemed as if the Run for the Roses, like so much else in those days, would disappoint. The press tried to heighten expectations by pitching the Derby as a battle between East and West, with the eastern Ladysman taking on the Kentuckian Head Play. The purse remained at $50,000, but missing was the usual level of anticipation for the Derby.

In the end, however, the 1933 Derby delivered excitement. The winner broke his maiden that day in a duel so close that most spectators could not tell who won. But it was the battling jockeys' pugilistic behavior and a photograph that captured their actions that made the "Fighting Finish" a race to remember.

Jockey Don Meade was only eighteen, and colleague Herb Fisher was about twenty-two as they headed into the 1933 Derby. Fisher, a British-born Canadian who became a jockey in 1926, had the ride on the favored Head Play. Californian Don Meade, although reputed to be a rising star, was aboard the less illustrious Brokers Tip. The Monday before the Derby, Churchill Downs stewards suspended Meade for rough riding on a horse named Sweepbrush. That suspension did not include contracts to ride in stakes races, allowing him to ride in the Derby. But Meade had been the only jockey suspended so far in the Churchill meet, and it foreshadowed his involvement in the Derby fight to come.

As the Derby drew nearer, bettors turned away from their original choice of W.R. Coe's colt Ladysman and toward Head Play as the favorite. Because Ladysman's sire, Pompey, was a sprinter whom Bubbling Over had beaten in the 1926 Derby, people believed Pompey's son would also prove unfit for the Derby distance. But they liked Head Play, a stocky chestnut by Man o' War's brother Mad Play. A *Blood-Horse* correspondent saw the colt's grandsire in him and called him "a typical Fair Play in conformation … he appeared the sturdiest horse in the field. Especially impressive were his deep, sloping shoulders, his superb head, and his confident demeanor."

Ex-jockey Willie Crump paid $550 for Head Play as a yearling, a bargain for a horse with his pedigree even in the cash-strapped 1930s. Crump brought the horse home only to find out that his intended owner did not want the colt after all. So Crump kept and trained Head Play. As a two-year-old, Head Play proved Crump's faith well-founded. He won the Hawthorne Juvenile and the Cincinnati Trophy.

Brokers Tip did not have the same history of wins as his rival Head Play. Bettors paid little attention to him although he was owned by the beloved millionaire "Colonel" (the title was

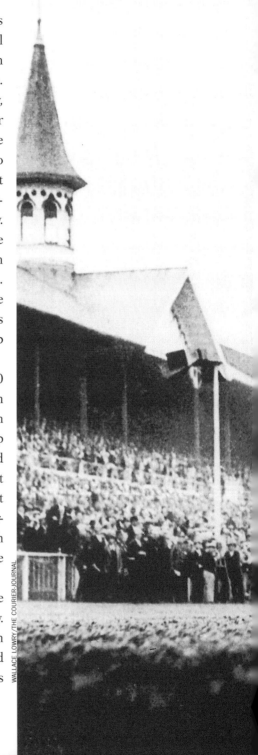

Wallace Lowry's photo of the 1933 Kentucky Derby shows the jockeys aboard Brokers Tip (right) and Head Play "fighting" to the wire

honorific) E.R. Bradley, a former prospector and bookie. Bradley owned gambling halls and was well known for his philanthropy. He had won the Derby with Behave Yourself in 1921, Bubbling Over in 1926, and Burgoo King in 1932. Bradley was trying for his fourth Derby win with Brokers Tip, another of his "B" horses carrying his green-and-white colors. (Bradley's practice of starting his horses' names with the letter B paid tribute to a horse he had purchased in 1899 named Bad News. This colt was so named in the hope that bad news travels fast, which turned out to be the case.) With a victory, Bradley's Idle Hour Farm would garner not only a fourth Derby, but also two in a row.

Brokers Tip, medium-sized and fairly long through the barrel, was, like 1924 Kentucky Derby winner Black Gold, a son of Bradley's Black Toney. Brokers Tip's dam was Forteresse by Sardanapale, who had won the French Derby. The Bradley colt looked more like his dam's side of the family and suffered their same ills, with leg problems such as a malformed foot and a calcium deficiency as a weanling. Olin Gentry, who worked for Bradley at Idle Hour Stock Farm, told Peter Chew in his *The Kentucky Derby: The First 100 Years* that he left the colt in a stall for two weeks with a brace on to reshape the foot and had one side of his horseshoe built up with leather. Brokers Tip's knees, however, were chronically sore.

Brokers Tip had yet to break his maiden when he started in the 1933 Derby but he had been third (to winner Head Play) at two in Latonia's Cincinnati Trophy, and earlier in his three-year-old season he had finished second to Warren Jr. in the Prospect Purse at the Lexington Association track. Also, Brokers Tip worked the Derby distance of a mile and a quarter in 2:08 3/5 the Wednesday before the race. These performances showed the colt had promise and reinforced Bradley's confidence in him.

As for Head Play, the Preparation Purse (also called the Derby Trial Purse and the forerunner of the Derby Trial Stakes) finalized his preeminence as a Derby contender. Seven of the eventual Derby entrants were present for the prep race, held at Churchill Downs on a rainy May 2. The muddy track was slow, upgraded from heavy ear-

THE BLOOD-HORSE

**Brokers Tip's only victory came in the Derby**

lier in the day. Head Play was rambunctious in the post and had trouble at the start, but he handily passed a Bradley horse named Boilermaker in the stretch. Head Play won by two lengths over the sprinter Isaiah, getting the mile in a respectable 1:39 2/5, considering the track's condition.

Head Play came out of that race with a cut on his left hind leg. Because a western champion, Burning Blaze, had been sidelined for the previous year's Derby with a cut leg, fans worried that Head Play would not be ready. Head Play's injury, however, didn't seem as serious, and he was seen as a possible Derby victor even with his injury. "West's Chief Hope Triumphs in Field of Ten Eligibles at Churchill Downs," read a *New York Times* headline the day after the race.

As Head Play's successes mounted, Crump was not the only horseman who understood the colt's potential. A partnership called Warm Stable, made up of Silas R. Mason and Arnold Hanger, offered Crump $30,000 for the colt. The decision to sell was difficult, as Crump had come so far with the horse, but Depression-era economics won out. Mrs. Mason chose new colors of orange-and-black for the Derby. Crump was still to saddle Head Play as well as collect $7,500 of the winnings if the colt won. After the Derby, however, T.P. Hayes, who had trained the 1913 Derby winner Donerail, was to take over training.

The reaches of the Depression had muted Louisville's usually festive atmosphere Derby week. Another shadow extended over horse racing when a jockey from Nebraska named Bernard "Buddy" Hanford, who had a mount in the Derby, died at Pimlico on May 3. His horse, Apprehensive, tripped in the backstretch of the sixth race, throwing Hanford to the ground, where he was crushed by the rest of the field. He was rushed to the hospital but died of multiple skull fractures. Hanford's mount for the Derby would have been Trace Call, who ended up being scratched with a fever.

Years later Hanford's younger brother Ira, also known as Babe, won the Kentucky Derby aboard Bold Venture, and another brother, Carl, became the trainer of five-time Horse of the Year Kelso.

The weather seemed to add to the gloom. Rain fell the two days prior to the Derby, and even when the sun beat down heavily for a while the second afternoon, the track remained muddy. The rain returned again that evening. Since none of the favorites were mudders, everyone hoped the forecast for clear weather and a fairly firm track would prove accurate. "Head Play To Be Hampered If Going Heavy," read one headline.

Derby Day was overcast, but the pall seemed to lift. The Derby itself still drew a crowd of 40,000. "Today," wrote Associated Press reporter Alan Gould, "with many of the leaders of State and Nation assembled for the fifty-ninth renewal at the sprawling, picturesque Churchill Downs, the Derby became something more than a traditional symbol. It was hailed as the banner bearer of a mighty effort to rescue the turf's sagging structure of public support, the turning point for a racing 'new deal.'"

James Roosevelt, son of President Franklin D. Roosevelt, and Mrs. Woodrow Wilson attended the race, and Postmaster General James A. Farley came to present the winner with the gold cup. Extra Pullman cars had been added to trains along the L&N railroad to accommodate Derby crowds. Poorer fans were "trusting to past performance in their hopes they will be able to crash the gate and fences, despite the announcement by Churchill Downs officials that strong barriers of iron and brawn will be raised against their assault." Churchill Downs looked beautiful, with all its flowers blooming in the springtime air.

The crowd reflected all walks of life, wrote Mary Elizabeth Plummer in the Louisville *Courier-Journal*. There were "well-groomed men and sleek women, hard boots who play their money on the tracks of the world, sun-browned people who met at Miami and who will meet again at Pimlico." For the first time in fifteen years, beer was served at the race, as Kentucky had lifted Prohibition. "The amber fluid got three thirsty cheers from thousands of dry throats," one reporter wrote.

Thirteen colts went to the post. The track had dried out by the afternoon and was rated good, upgraded from slow in the morning, very much as it had been for Brokers Tip's excellent work three days before. The Derby was the sixth race on an eight-race card, and post time was 5:10.

Moments before the race Dark Winter and then Head Play became rambunctious. Head Play's antics harkened back to those of his fractious grandsire Fair Play and led to the race's being delayed eight minutes. William Hamilton, the starter, was just telling jockeys to "take it easy" when one of the

**Don Meade**

jockeys cracked his whip, and Head Play, Mr. Khayyam, Strideaway, and Dark Winter jumped at the sound. Hamilton admonished the jockeys. Dark Winter, who was causing even more trouble than Head Play, was led to the outside post of the starting gate, and almost the second he settled in, the gate sprung open.

At the start the sprinter Isaiah, who had been second to Head Play in the Preparation Purse, was out front with Good Advice, Head Play, Kerry Patch, Dark Winter, and Ladsyman right behind him. Isaiah and Good Advice held the lead with Head Play right behind them and Brokers Tip remaining on the outside as the field went down the homestretch for the first time.

Head Play took the lead as they came into the backstretch, with Isaiah and Good Advice right behind. Near him were Charley O., Kerry Patch, and Ladysman. Although Brokers Tip was gaining ground, it looked as if only Charley O. had any chance of catching Head Play out in front.

Turning for home, Brokers Tip sat a full length behind Head Play. He passed Charley O. a quarter-mile from the finish. Fisher brought Head Play into the straightaway, swerving out, and pushed Charley O. wide, avoiding the mushy going near the rail. All three horses — Head Play, Charley O., and Brokers Tip — raced on together. But now Meade found room to bring Brokers Tip up right next to the rail. Charley O. fell back, leaving just Head Play and Brokers Tip to battle it out. "Then," *The Blood-Horse* wrote, "ensued one of the most regrettable incidents in the history of the Kentucky Derby … Through the last three-sixteenths of a mile the contest was not a horse race so much as a hand-to-hand combat between the jockeys."

Because the fighting finish took place before the days of cameras recording multiple angles, no one will ever know exactly what happened as the jockeys fought their way down the stretch. "It looked as though they were locked together," wrote Alan Gould of the Associated Press. "The dark Bradley horse on the inside, the chestnut Head Play on the outside, both close to the rail. At least twice Fisher was seen to lash out as he sought to lift his horse ahead or break loose from the deadlock. They were still so close together as they passed the finish that it might have been a dead heat, or a victory for either colt so far as most observers were concerned."

At the moment the horses crossed the finish line, Head Play's head was oddly canted toward the right because Fisher was gripping Head Play's right rein tightly as he leaned left to hang onto Brokers Tip's saddle pad. Once the horses crossed the line, Fisher switched his crop to his left hand and hit Meade with it. It had not been a particularly fast Derby at 2:06 4/5, five whole seconds shy of the record, but considering the footing and the fighting, there was no shame for Brokers Tip in his time.

Directly after the race Fisher kept Head Play galloping until he got to the stewards. He ran up to the judge's stand to lodge his foul claim — he said that Meade had started everything when he grabbed his saddlecloth — but the judges did not appear to listen. "Evidently," said *The Blood-Horse,* "they had seen something of what happened and had already made up their mind there was to be no disqualification." They literally turned their backs on him, and Fisher sat down and cried.

THE COURIER-JOURNAL

**Herb Fisher**

Meanwhile, the stewards officially declared Brokers Tip the winner. Meade went to have his picture taken. He was so flustered after the fracas that reporters could not understand him and made him repeat that he was "glad to have been the Kentucky Derby winner and ride Brokers Tip for Mr. Bradley.

"I knew Brokers Tip had it won three-eighths from the finish," Meade added. Bradley gave Meade 10 percent of the Derby winnings, so the jockey walked away from the fray with $4,892.

But the fighting finish was not yet over. As Meade stepped into the jockeys' room, Fisher lunged at him with fists flying. Meade shielded himself from the flailing, with Fisher never landing a blow. A valet and Louisville reporter John Herchenroeder pried him away from Meade. Fisher kept crying, "He beat me out of it; he beat me out of it."

The fight demanded that the Churchill Downs stewards mete out punishment to both Fisher and Meade. The trial deciding the penalties

was held on May 8, the Monday after the race. Jockey Charles Corbett, who had been riding Charley O., testified first. Then Meade and, finally, Fisher were questioned. Possibly because of the furor surrounding the fight, the entire hearing was held behind closed doors, so reporters had to wait for the judges' handwritten ruling to be issued. The stewards suspended Meade for thirty days. Fisher got thirty days plus five extra because he instigated the fight in the jockeys' room. The stewards said, "Each boy, according to the evidence and observation, was guilty of grasping the equipment of the other. Jockey Fisher was given an additional five days for assaulting jockey Meade while in the jockeys' quarters after the race."

Wallace Lowry, a staff photographer for the *Louisville Times* and *The Courier-Journal*, took the famous photograph that helped people visualize what had happened. Lowry had been lying on the ground, right under the inside rail. Like any photographer in 1933, he only had one chance to take a great photo of the finish. (In *Derby Fever*, Jim Bolus writes that there was a long-standing rumor that Lowry, like

THE BLOOD-HORSE

**Head Play would go on to win the Preakness**

many Derby revelers, had had one too many, and that's why he was lying down.)

The photo clearly shows Meade's right hand hanging onto Fisher's shoulder, and Fisher's left hand grabbing Brokers Tip's saddlecloth. Both jockeys were leaning toward each other. It was obvious that both jockeys had behaved badly.

A newsreel showed that Fisher started the fray by grabbing Brokers Tip's saddlecloth right when Meade put Brokers Tip on the rail. Brokers Tip tried twice to move off, but both times Fisher grabbed the pad. Meade fought back, grabbing Fisher's shoulder. According to the Associated Press, the newsreel showed that Fisher hit Meade with his crop "near the finish."

In a note in columnist Old Rosebud's weekly piece, *The Blood-Horse*'s editor responded with surprise to a reader's idea that Fisher struck Meade before the finish. It was clearly a confusing couple of seconds; years later Meade said, "He hit me with the whip after the finish, but not before. His reins were dangling perhaps the last sixteenth of a mile. If he'd just ridden his horse, he'd have won by two or three lengths." Yet Bolus writes that Fisher said, "I hit him across the head with my whip once or twice before the finish and then after the finish."

With all this confusion, reporters still had a little trouble deciding what to make of the Fisher-Meade debacle. The newspaper reporting started out favoring Meade. Despite his reputation for fighting, as the Derby-winning jockey, they took his side, and because many believed that Fisher had started the fight, Meade seemed to be a sympathetic figure. The Associated Press called him "understandingly flustered … as he had just been subjected to fisticuffs by a ragingly disappointed jockey who claimed Meade had fouled him during the race."

Publications with a bit more time to digest what had happened saw things in clearer detail. "What the crowd saw was fully as thrilling as anything it had previously seen in a Kentucky Derby renewal, but not quite so glorious," *The Blood-Horse*'s reporter wrote in understatement. "What kept the two horses running on such even terms through the last eighth of a mile may have been the fact that their riders … were engaged in a hand-to-hand struggle which included leg locking, saddle-cloth grabbing, bumping and slashing with whips, and which did not terminate until the two riders had engaged in a fist fight in the jockeys' room after the race." (Later, it seemed that no leg locking had actually occurred, but that all the other acts chronicled did take place.)

Race fans fought almost as bitterly as Meade and Fisher about who should have won the Derby. Because rough riding was more common in those days, some people saw nothing wrong with Meade's actions. Like today's professional hockey fans, some sanctioned fighting as part of the sport. The *Lexington Leader* compiled some reader responses, among them, "What I would like to know is what you would have done in Meade's place or had him do, pull up and say, 'go on, you old meanie'? … There was nothing for Meade to do but to fend him off or go over the fence." Brownie Leach, a columnist for the paper, responded that the spot did not look so tight from the press box. He allowed that Brokers Tip would, however, probably have had to pull up if Meade had not pushed Head Play away. Leach called for stiffer punishment for rough riding in general, though. "Make the jockeys stick to their business of riding," he wrote.

*The Blood-Horse*'s columnist, Old Rosebud, noted, "The trainers of every Eastern-owned Thoroughbred in the race with whom the writer has discussed the running also are of the opinion that the best horse was second." Many maintained that if Fisher had not pushed Charley O. wide and made Head Play veer away from his spot on the rail, Brokers Tip could not have come up on the inside. Then Head Play would have outrun him before the finish.

Lost in the commotion over the Fisher-Meade battle was the racing history made as Colonel Bradley won his fourth Derby. Racing fans were happy for Bradley and enjoyed his victory. Noting how delighted race fans seemed for the Colonel, *The Courier-Journal* reported that "the crowd likes to say 'Bradley's horse.' " Also, Brokers Tip was the first maiden to win the Derby since Sir Barton, in 1919. Since Sir Barton had gone on from his maiden win in the Derby to take the Triple Crown, Brokers Tip fans hoped he would do the same.

## Kentucky Derby
## Purse: $50,000 Added

**6th Race  Churchill Downs - May 6, 1933. Fifty-ninth running Kentucky Derby**
Purse $50,000 added. Three-year-olds. 1 1-4 Miles. Main Track. Track: Good.
Net value to winner, $48,925 and gold trophy; second, $6,000; third, $3,000; fourth, $1,000.

| Horse | A | Wgt | Eqp | Odds | PP | 1/4 | 1/2 | 3/4 | 1 | Str | Fin | Jockey |
|---|---|---|---|---|---|---|---|---|---|---|---|---|
| Brokers Tip | 3 | 126 | wb | 8.93 | 11 | 11 | $11^1$ | $8^x$ | $4^2$ | $2^{1x}$ | $1^{no}$ | D Meade |
| Head Play | 3 | 126 | w | 5.64 | 7 | 5 | $3^x$ | $1^x$ | $1^1$ | $1^h$ | $2^4$ | H W Fisher |
| Charley O. | 3 | 126 | wb | 6.02 | 1 | 6 | $7^h$ | $6^1$ | $2^{1x}$ | $3^4$ | $3^{1x}$ | C Corbett |
| Ladysman | 3 | 126 | wb | ‡1.43 | 4 | 7 | $5^x$ | $7^3$ | $5^{1x}$ | $5^{1x}$ | $4^{no}$ | R Workman |
| Pomponius | 3 | 126 | w | ‡ | 12 | 12 | $10^x$ | $9^{1x}$ | $6^x$ | $6^3$ | $5^3$ | J Bejshak |
| Spicson | 3 | 126 | wb | †25.85 | 9 | 13 | 13 | $12^3$ | $10^{1x}$ | $7^1$ | $6^{1x}$ | R Fischer |
| Kerry Patch | 3 | 126 | wb | 26.89 | 5 | 1 | $6^{1x}$ | $5^x$ | $3^h$ | $4^h$ | $7^2$ | L Schaefer |
| Mr. Khayyam | 3 | 126 | w | §4.09 | 13 | 9 | $9^1$ | $11^3$ | $9^h$ | $9^2$ | $8^x$ | P Walls |
| Inlander | 3 | 126 | wb | 44.27 | 6 | 8 | $8^2$ | $10^2$ | $8^1$ | $8^2$ | $9^{1x}$ | D Bellizzi |
| Strideaway | 3 | 126 | wb | † | 8 | 4 | $12^x$ | 13 | $12^3$ | $10^3$ | $10^5$ | A Beck |
| Dark Winter | 3 | 126 | wb | † | 3 | 10 | $4^2$ | $4^h$ | $7^2$ | $11^8$ | $11^{12}$ | R Jones |
| Isaiah | 3 | 126 | wb | 66.86 | 10 | 2 | $2^{1x}$ | $3^x$ | $11^2$ | $12^8$ | 12 | C McCrossen |
| Good Advice | 3 | 126 | wb | § | 2 | 3 | $1^h$ | $2^h$ | 13 | 13 | P. up | E Legere |

† Mutuel field. ‡ Coupled as W. R. Coe entry; § Catawba Stable entry.

**Off Time:** 5:18  **Time Of Race:** :23½  :47½  1:12½  1:40¾  2:06½
**Start:** Good For All  **Track:** Good
**Equipment::** w for whip; b for blinkers

**Mutuel Payoffs**

| 11 | Brokers Tip | $19.86 | $6.28 | $4.54 |
|---|---|---|---|---|
| 7 | Head Play | | 5.52 | 4.08 |
| 1 | Charley O. | | | 3.84 |

**Winner:** Brokers Tip, br. c. by Black Toney—Forteresse, by Sardanapale (Trained by H. J. Thompson).
Bred by Idle Hour Stock Farm in Ky.

**Start good out of machine. Won driving; second and third the same.**
BROKERS TIP, much the best, began very slowly, saved some ground when moving up leaving the backstretch, but lost some on the stretch turn, then went to the inside and, responding to urging and overcoming interference, was up to win in the final strides after a long and rough drive. HEAD PLAY, rated close to the pace, went to the front easily, came out when increasing his lead on the stretch turn and bumped the winner when holding on stubbornly. CHARLEY O., well in hand for three-quarters, challenged gamely, then tired, but held LADYSMAN safe. The latter raced wide most of the way, was under restraint for seven-eighths and failed to rally when hard urged. POMPONIUS closed resolutely. SPICSON began slowly. KERRY PATCH tired. MR. KHAYYAM was never a factor. ISAIAH and DARK WINTER showed early speed. GOOD ADVICE quit badly and was pulled up.
Scratched—Pompoleon, 126; Sarada, 126; Fingal, 126; Warren Jr., 126; Captain Red, 126; Boilermaker, 126; Silent Shot, 126; At Top, 121; Fair Rochester, 126.

**Owners:** (1) E R Bradley; (2) Mrs S B Mason; (3) R M Eastman estate; (4) W R Coe; (5) W R Coe; (6) L M Severson; (7) L Rosenberg; (8) Catawba Stable; (9) Brookmeade Stable; (10) Three D's Stock Farm Stable; (11) W S Kilmer; (12) J W Parrish; (13) Catawba Stable
©EQUIBASE

But Head Play went on to win the Preakness with Charlie Kurtsinger up. He also won the San Juan Capistrano and Suburban handicaps. Brokers Tip's old leg infirmities plagued him, and he finished last in the 1933 Preakness. Brokers Tip never won another race or even finished in the money again. Many had said, even before the Preakness, that if Fisher had just done his job on Derby Day instead of worrying about Meade, he would have won the Derby. The Preakness seemed to bear this out.

Although he won the Derby, Meade lost much in later years due to unlawful behavior. He was a talented rider, and his career had promise. In 1939 and again in 1941, he led all American jockeys in races won, but in 1937 he was ruled off for betting against his own horses, then was reinstated a year later, and in 1942 he was suspended six months for collusion in interfering with the running of a race. By 1945 he was not even allowed a license in either the United States or Mexico. After his riding career ended, Meade trained some racehorses and owned bars.

In 1983 Meade and Fisher, who were by then sixty-nine and seventy-two years old, respectively, and both living in Florida, attended the Derby for the fiftieth anniversary of their race. Although they did not exchange a word for fifteen years after the Fighting Finish, they eventually did become cordial, linked forever in Lowry's famous photograph. In his later years Meade said: "We grabbed, grabbed, grabbed all through the stretch. It was the survival of the fittest. I couldn't sit there and let him rough me around and not do nothing about it … I'm not blaming him for trying to do what he did because in those days that's what you did. If you didn't do it, you wasn't a race rider." Meade died in 1996.

Fisher, who died in 1983, never gave up on Head Play. He once told a reporter that three of the four stewards told him Head Play had won, and that Brokers Tip won simply because he was a Bradley horse. "Bradley was the king of Kentucky in those days … Gave hundreds of thousands to charity. No way they weren't going to give it to him. If that had been me on his horse, I'd have won it … I had got beat on the best horse, and I had got out-roughed — and I was pretty rough myself."

Both jockeys seemed to think about the fighting finish until the end of their lives, bearing out a prediction made in the June 10, 1933, issue of *The Blood-Horse* that "very likely all the present generation will have passed the way of all flesh ere the matter shall cease to be a subject for talk in connection with Kentucky Derby history." In just a few seconds, desperation and violence ignited to make the race unforgettable. The 1933 Kentucky Derby will live on as a symbol of the grueling days of Depression-era racing, and a story of the desire to win at any cost.

*By Eliza R.L. McGraw*

# A Dream Derby
## (Black Gold, 1924)

THE FLIES WERE EVERYWHERE in Juarez that time of year. Bothersome. Not much different than the racing officials who, jabbering in Spanish, had the trainer surrounded. Imagine the nerve, telling a man what he had to do with his own horse. All this commotion over an eight hundred-dollar claiming race. It just didn't make any sense.

Something told him he was in deep trouble. Another voice told him not to back down. So he just stood there, leaning his elbows on the counter of the racing office, and pinched a wad of chewing tobacco into his jaw, set tight for the discussion ahead. The track owners didn't even have a ceiling fan in this God-forsaken hole in the wall. What a dump. He should never have brought his mare down to Mexico in the first place. On the other hand, the money was good, and the little mare was as quick as a Texas tornado.

They pulled the book out on him. It was a brown leather book, and it was up on a shelf with other legal stuff and papers that they said were the law and written by important people up in New York and Kentucky. They went over it word by word. The horseman pretended to be listening, but the truth was that he didn't care. Paragraph something or other. Section this or that. So what? As far as he was concerned, they could take their rules and shove them where the sun don't shine.

He could hear the other trainer, some guy named Ramsey, arguing with the stewards in another room. Ramsey was demanding that he had put in a good claim and the mare was his fair and square. The more the trainer heard Ramsey talk about the rules of racing, the hotter he got. He considered walking into that room and pulling the guy

into the parking lot and settling it once and for all with bare knuckles.

Finally, like a dry twig, his patience snapped. They could read from their books and point and threaten him all they wanted. His mind was made up. Without saying another word, he stormed out of the racing office and walked back to the barn. He sat down on a bucket in front of the mare's stall, and with a loaded shotgun cradled on his lap, Al Hoots waited for them to come.

He did not have to wait long. Toby Ramsey's groom arrived with a lead shank to take Useeit to her new barn. Taking notice of the double-barreled shotgun, the groom backed off to live another day. The next wave brought an assembly of coats and ties that managed to get half way down the shed row, close enough to hear the sound of the safety lever on the shotgun click from left to right. Alfred Worth Hoots was tired of talking.

**Black Gold wearing the blanket of roses**

Hoots was more than just fond of his nine-year-old race mare Useeit; he was in love with his breadwinner who had won thirty-four races from 122 starts at county fairs in Oklahoma, at recognized tracks in Kansas and Texas, and at any Sunday morning tumbleweed patch of match race they could find in between. Hoots was not about to give her up. Seeing the trainer dig in with the shotgun, the officials retreated. Safely back at their desks, they wrote up the documentation that would ban Hoots from racing across all jurisdictions in North America.

The next morning Hoots loaded Useeit onto a boxcar. They headed home, back to the short-grass prairie country of northeast Oklahoma. If he couldn't race Useeit, they couldn't stop him from breeding her. The year was 1916. As owner or trainer, Al Hoots would never see another racetrack. No regrets. He still had the horse that he had discovered and come to love.

But over time the hurt inside wore on him and his health declined. The racing, the excitement and competition were over. Nothing could replace it. Life as he had lived it was finished.

One thing they couldn't take away was that when it came to horses, Al Hoots possessed a third eye. He could see something in horses that others missed. Hoots first took notice of Useeit at a fairgrounds meet outside of Chickasaw, Oklahoma, in May of 1909. No bigger than a pony and chunky around the girth, the filly had more than obscure parentage. Her pedigree (by Bonnie Joe out of Effie M.) might as well have read: Garbage Can out of Slow Motion. Hoots could have cared less that she was the butt of all jokes. He was convinced she was special.

Several match races were run that day, and in the finale, Useeit flashed speed through a hell-raising gauntlet of Cherokee and Osage Indians as they threw their stovepipe hats into the wind. Useeit was caught in the last jump at the wire by an older, fashionably bred mare, but Hoots was pleased. The little fireball had heart and durability. Unable to pay with cash, Hoots offered up eighty acres of grazing land and bought the Oklahoma-bred on the spot.

Useeit was put out for rest and grazing. Hoots guarded over her, worked with her, built up the muscle in her rear engine, and watched as she filled out. The layers of limestone under the hardscrabble earth on the Hoots' ranch would twist a plowshare like a pretzel, but the short grass seemed to supply the right prescription for sound bone. Back on the bullring tracks and straightaways, Useeit began to win. Three strides past five furlongs and she was looking for the barn, but Useeit always gave her best.

After the trip to Juarez, Hoots took to spending long hours alone on the prairie. For a while he tinkered down at the quarry that had supplied the stone for his house. Mustering as much enthusiasm as possible, he made repairs to the barn that was now empty of horses — except for one mare the color of mud. One thread of hope held him together: breeding Useeit to a prominent Kentucky sire named Black Toney. Acquired by E.R. Bradley as a yearling, the fashionably bred Black Toney was a respectable racehorse and proved an exceptional stallion for his owner's Idle Hour Stock Farm, ultimately siring forty stakes winners. Hoots' dream to breed Useeit to Black Toney refused to fade. With his health spiraling downward, Hoots (who would die within a year of the incident in Juarez) repeated the breeding plan again and again to his wife, Rosa.

Al and Rosa Hoots made for a curious couple when they married in 1886. At the time, both husband and wife were considered second-class citizens: a never-give-up Irishman with strains of Choctaw in his blood and a seventeen-year-old girl whose mother was full-blooded Osage Indian and whose father was a French sea captain. Al Hoots was tenacious as a bulldog, but he suffered in comparison to Rosa, who had been weaned on adversity.

Al and Rosa had settled on a ranch outside of Skiatook (translation from the Osage language: deer standing by the creek), Oklahoma, and had begun raising cattle. Waves of settlers and pioneers had deemed the barren land worthless, but it was a sacred refuge to Rosa. For Rosa's mother, Jane More Captain, the hill country around Skiatook had been the end of a long, forced march of her ancestors that had originated in Ohio. Broken treaty after broken treaty drove the Osage

**Rosa Hoots, trainer Hanley Webb (second from left), and jockey J.D. Mooney
after the Derby trophy presentation**

nation westward into Missouri. After a temporary relocation in Kansas, the last stop was the Indian Territory that would soon become Oklahoma.

By federal mandate the reservation was off limits to U.S. government marshals and local sheriffs. Not necessarily a blessing. Cattle rustlers, outlaws, and thieves used the reservation for sanctuary, requiring Rosa (when it was her turn) to sleep at night under the stars in culverts out on the open range of the Osage Hills. With a saddle for a pillow and a loaded rifle under her blanket, she kept watch on the herd. Each spring she rode out on cattle drives to Kansas City and Omaha, attending to a string of cutting horses under her care. By the ninth grade she had dropped out of the Catholic mission school on the reservation. Algebra and world history would have to wait.

Other girls were satisfied with learning to weave and cook, but not Rosa. Her pride kept her from entering the cocoon of depression she witnessed among the majority of reservation Indians. She developed a sharp mind for business. Rosa would stay close to her father, who was the tribe's interpreter, in his council talks with the elders and listen with a keen ear about his trips to Washington, D.C. Following her mother's Indian heritage, Rosa Hoots grew to appreciate that a dream or vision was to be taken seriously — never to be neglected or ignored. She understood the teaching that beyond each mountain there is another mountain. Keep walking forward, keep climbing, keep the vow alive. It was the way of her people.

After Al died, Rosa experienced more hard times, and she had several opportunities to sell Useeit. No way. Holding fast to his last wishes to breed the mare to a Kentucky stallion, Rosa kept the mare under her wing. In 1917, after several dry holes, a gusher erupted on the parcel of reservation land Hoots had leased from the Osage Nation. Within two years 17 percent of the crude oil marketed in the United States was coming out of fields in Oklahoma. Rosa Hoots was suddenly wealthy, and she could finally make her husband's wish become reality. Useeit was sent to Colonel E.R. Bradley's Idle Hour Stock Farm in Lexington, Kentucky, for a mating with Al's choice — Black Toney.

On February 17, 1921, in an open meadow off Old Frankfort Pike near Lexington, Useeit gave birth to a colt. Coal black, the baby did not look like Useeit from any angle. The foal received the blood of the prominent Domino line from his sire and from day one had the look of a racehorse. Rosa Hoots named him Black Gold. It was the Indians' term for the oil that gushed from the Osage soil.

Despite strong objections of friends and advice from horsemen, Rosa Hoots picked a former ranch hand, Hanley Webb, to train Black Gold. Positive attributes to Webb's character and personality were difficult to uncover. He was a confirmed loner, overweight and bow-legged, and never met a fifth of gin that he didn't like. Prior to his stint of employment as a cattle hand on the Hootses' ranch, Webb had a brief career as a lawman. Whatever his obscure past, one thing was certain — he thought it was a mistake to coddle a horse.

In the spring of 1922, Webb was dispatched to Lexington where his first act was to take the yearling off the farm and stable him in a barn at the Kentucky Association racetrack. Webb had Black Gold exercised, cow-pasture style, on a lunge line. If this method worked for wild mustangs, it was good enough for Thoroughbreds. When Black Gold kept running away and proved difficult to break, Webb retained an Osage Indian named Chief Johnson to apply more heavy-handed tactics. At least on the surface, Johnson's punishment seemed to work.

Rain or shine, Webb and Johnson put Black Gold through a hammer and anvil ordeal. Whatever didn't kill the colt would make him stronger seemed to be the logic. Marathon gallops (sometimes twice a day) were popular with Johnson. The rotund Webb would even ride Black Gold himself. Late at night when the impulse to drink and play cards at a nearby saloon hit him, Webb would often choose Black Gold as his means of transportation.

At Fair Grounds in New Orleans on January 8, 1923, Black Gold made the first start of his career, demolishing a full field of two-year-old maidens. Blowing horses away, he won two of his next three allowance races. In an allowance race at Jefferson Park, Black Gold set a track record for three and a half furlongs. Word spread. There was a racehorse in town. When reporters showed up at the barn, Webb, with a cigar clamped between his toothless gums, bragged that he owned Black Gold.

As Black Gold's reputation grew, he attracted the attention of one of the top New Orleans riders. J.D. "Sit Still" Mooney. The uneducated son of a Mississippi River barge hand, Mooney from the age of nine had supported his mother by working in a livery stable. His life revolved around a riding circuit of Louisiana in the winter, Kentucky and Illinois in the spring, and Canada in the summer.

But in the early months of 1923, Mooney became transfixed with obtaining the mount on the promising juvenile. The jockey began watching Webb's every move and listening to his every word. He wanted the mount on Black Gold and was convinced that Webb was holding back.

Mooney rarely let Black Gold out of his sight. The jockey, who had been aboard such stakes and handicap horses as Display, Whiskaway, and Fire Brand, was convinced that Black Gold possessed considerable promise, and he affixed himself to the colt like gravy on rice. The jockey became hesitant to accept other mounts, fearing that a suspension or injury could leave him on the sidelines. Like clockwork Mooney showed up at the barn before dawn to help groom and exercise the colt and never went to bed without topping off the water bucket. On his off days he would drive out to the country in his Model T and cut clover with a hand sickle, filling up the passenger seat and bringing the special treat back to the barn.

At the conclusion of the Fair Grounds meet, Webb decided it was time to send Black Gold up to the big leagues. At a railroad spur within walking distance of the track, Black Gold was loaded onto a boxcar for the long trip to Churchill Downs. Rather than sleep in the Pullman car, Rosa Hoots, who liked to ride with the colt when he traveled from track to track, bedded down with a cushion of straw and a blanket to accompany her colt north. All dressed up and somewhere to go, Mooney, in hopes of riding Black Gold, hit the highway in his car and drove, without sleep, to Louisville.

At Churchill Downs, Black Gold got his taste for stakes competition. On the same afternoon that Zev won the 1923 Kentucky Derby, Black Gold whipped a top-flight field of two-year-olds in the Bashford Manor Stakes. Chopped up in heavy traffic, Black Gold recovered and made up a ton of ground to win going away. From the sidelines Mooney watched and bided his time. Seven more races he waited.

Finally, Mooney's devotion to the little black colt reaped its reward. The smitten jockey piloted Black Gold for the first time, a winning effort in the Catlettsburg Purse at old Latonia in northern Kentucky.

His perseverance having paid off, Mooney knew where his bread was buttered, and he was determined that Black Gold would carry assigned weight and not an ounce over. To control his weight, Mooney pushed himself to the threshold of exhaustion. Wearing a custom-made rubber suit, he tied a rope around his waist and then ran six miles each evening behind a moving car.

With Black Gold he rode with shortened stirrups and typically let the horse run as he liked (mid-pack or trailing) until after about three-

H.C. ASHBY

**Black Gold at Fair Grounds for his first start at two**

quarters of a mile when he would suggest a quicker pace with a slight tap of the whip. From this point, horse and rider preferred to give chase to one or two contenders until settling the argument in mid-stretch and pulling away. Whatever the style, Mooney and Black Gold just clicked.

On November 13 Mooney and Black Gold cruised to an easy victory in the New Albany Purse at Churchill Downs to conclude the colt's juvenile season. It was an eleven-month, eighteen-race campaign in which Black Gold won nine races and placed second five times and third twice. The colt was favored in at least fourteen of his eighteen starts. Owned by an Indian woman from a reservation somewhere in Oklahoma and officially registered as "black" by The Jockey Club, Black Gold was becoming something of a national curiosity in the media. To racing fans he was a hero on the horizon.

Racehorses are unpredictable creatures. Who knows or understands how the ingredients of a racehorse can remix and ignite between the ages of two and three? From shoulder to rump, newly aligned muscles seem to spring and contract, ready to burst with collective energy. The neck arches, the ears prick, the morning tub of oats can't come quickly enough. Plodding around the shed row and dull shuffling of the feet are replaced with a bouncing gait. The churning and bubbling of blood, bone, and flesh in the thousand-pound petri dish of Black Gold in the spring of 1924 had combined to produce a horse on fire.

Treating his opposition like stepchildren, Black Gold opened his three-year-old season under Mooney on March 6 at Jefferson Park. Toying with allowance company, he won laughing under a choke hold. Black Gold won another top-level allowance race, and by then Mooney finally got Webb to admit that the long-range plan was the Kentucky Derby.

Trainer and jockey needed one more glimpse of evidence. One more nudge in the right direction. In the Louisiana Derby, facing several top colts from eastern stables, Black Gold showed he was in a class of his own. Carrying 126 pounds in a driving rain, Black Gold, breaking from an outside post, went to the lead at once and won by six lengths. The splattered competition jogged back to the unsaddling area dripping mud. Mooney's white pants were spotless. Preceded by a growing perception of him as a great racehorse, Black Gold shipped to Churchill Downs.

The long gallops continued, morning after morning, week after week. Four days before the Kentucky Derby, Black Gold won the Derby Trial Purse in a breeze by eight lengths. For anyone with the instinct to look and listen, Black Gold seemed to be saying "bring it on."

On the morning of May 17, the atmosphere in Louisville was electric. In the barrooms and barbershops, conversation centered around the conflict among the big name eastern establishment horses from the likes of the Whitneys, Colonel Bradley's three-horse entry, and the upstart Black Gold. It was not just another horse race. In fact, it was not just another Derby. It was the fiftieth. It was the "Golden Jubilee."

Special trains from Chicago, New York, Baltimore, and Philadelphia rolled into town, transforming the railroad yards into a colony of private parties. From all points of the compass, automobiles poured into the crowded neighborhood around the track. Boats from along the Ohio River moored at the docks to unload eager bettors. By eleven o'clock in the morning, the rickety old grandstand was being tested as a throng estimated in excess of 80,000 people packed the stands and depleted the available stock of bourbon intended for mint juleps.

The nail biting commenced at 4:37 p.m. when the horses left the paddock and stepped on the track. Played by a military band, Stephen Foster's "My Old Kentucky Home" replaced the "Star-Spangled Banner" that year for the post parade, beginning a popular tradition. From the first note to the last chorus, grown men were now allowed to cry.

After the warm-ups, the horses slowed to a jog then walked to the barrier at the head of the stretch. Black Gold had drawn post position number one. Without a starting gate, jockeys and handlers did their best to line the horses up in official order behind web netting strung across the track. Jittery and on the muscle, not all of the horses cooperated. In the milling about, Black Gold was bumped out of position. Mooney, keeping his horse relaxed, turned his mount away from the confusion and motioned for an assistant starter to lead Black Gold back to the rail where the colt planted his feet and stuck his nose into the webbing.

Seconds away from the start, Mooney grabbed the knotted reins and hunched down. Mrs. Walter Jeffords' Diogenes on the outside of the assembled pack broke under the barrier. He was led back and starter William Snyder waited for that one moment of stillness when no jockey was hollering for advantage and the field was more or less pointed in the right direction. Finally, the instant arrived, and Snyder jerked down the flag. The barrier flew up and nineteen of the best three-year-olds in the country exploded like a covey of startled quail. Quickest of all was Transmute (part of the H.P. Whitney entry) who cleared the field by daylight in the first two hundred yards. Bracadale, under the shrewd Earl Sande, came away alertly from post twelve and angled in sharply.

Just as there was no starting gate, there was no film patrol or instant replay in those days. Rules were for fools, and jockeys routinely grabbed bridles and saddle cloths, locked legs, or held on to tails to impede the progress of their competition. Herding the favorite out or boxing him in was common practice, and Black Gold was the public choice. A gasp came from the infield crowd that witnessed Bracadale slam Black Gold into the rail. Seeing their chance to bury Caesar, the jocks on Baffling, Chilhowee, and Wild Aster clustered around Black Gold, keeping him pinned down like a prisoner for the first quarter-mile.

Around the first turn the sleek and attractive Bracadale, with his low, long stride, made it look like lights out for the chase pack. Owned by oil man Harry Sinclair and trained by Sam Hildreth, the Rancocas Stable star — the second choice at 3-1 along with stablemate Mad Play — had seized the lead and was running easily. Greentree Stable's Wild Aster and Idle Hour's Baffling drafted behind. Like the annoying flies that had pestered Al Hoots back in Juarez, an unwanted escort of four kept Black Gold surrounded on the rail.

In the selective breeding of horses, you don't always get what you want. But sometimes you get what you need. Glancing up ahead, Mooney saw Bracadale, midway down the backstretch, aided by the wind at his back, stealing away. No time to wait. Mooney needed a burst of speed. He needed Useeit. At that precise instant Black Gold propelled himself between the bumping shoulders of Transmute and Chilhowee. Plunging through the narrow gap, he was free. Taking dead aim on the heels of the three horses ahead of him, Mooney maneuvered Black Gold into position.

The first turn had been about escaping from trouble. The second turn was going to be about causing some trouble. With the white shadow roll on his nose held high, Black Gold, three wide off the fence and clear of traffic, lengthened stride and cruised by Wild Aster. The crowd let out a roar, seeing that he was back in the fight. Only Bracadale and Baffling remained in front of him, and Baffling was tiring. Chilhowee, a 15-1 shot, moved with Black Gold around the turn. He angled down to secure the fence. With renewed interest Transmute pulled within striking distance.

140

From far back Altawood was throwing in a rally.

As the field turned for home, it could have been a chariot race in the Coliseum. Down a corridor of deafening noise, each horse had its own lane. Hugging the rail, Chilhowee shot to a short lead over Bracadale. With a quarter of a mile to go, Mooney, sitting still as his nickname suggested, fanned Black Gold out four wide, keeping the other two on a short leash. At that point, Black Gold had to answer a major question.

There's a reason they don't call it jockey racing. From the final black-and-white striped sixteenth pole to the wire, it would be up to Black Gold. In all their time together Mooney and the colt had never been closer. Approaching that final pole, Mooney leaned forward, pushing his fists into the neck of Black Gold, asking, hoping, for stamina. From beneath the thin leather saddle, Mooney felt the blood of Black Toney boil in the heart of his colt. With something left undiscovered, Black Gold threw in a furious attack, flying by the desperate Chilhowee in the last forty yards to win by a half-length over a closely bunched group.

No starting gate. No film patrol. No photo-finish camera. From the flying blur of heads, necks, and noses, the three placing judges had to determine the order of finish. Chilhowee was placed second by a nose. They ruled Idle Hour's Beau Butler (wearing green and white silks similar to those of Rancocas Stable's Bracadale) third when, in fact, he had finished far back after a tangled start. Bracadale was judged fifth, a nose and two heads behind Black Gold.

High in the clubhouse, Rosa Hoots stood up and said a polite farewell to the society ladies. Wearing a plain violet dress with a black straw hat pulled down tight over her head, the woman who as a young girl had lived in a lean-to shack next to a trading post was escorted down to the judge's stand to meet her horse and jockey. The applause lasted a full five minutes. Poised and dignified, she accepted the new gold trophy (worth five thousand dollars) with a bow. Then she did something even general manager Matt Winn was not prepared for. Keeping to tribal traditions, Rosa Hoots had come bearing gifts. She presented Winn with a box of his favorite cigars.

The winner's share of the 1924 Kentucky Derby was worth $52,775, but Hoots demanded Churchill Downs remit in cash. Selling coffee, flour, and utensils, and trading buffalo hides at the trading post on the reservation had taught her that the white man's credit, much less his government treaties, was often worthless. The money was eventually brought to her while she sat waiting and talking to Mooney's wife, Marjorie, outside the stable tackroom near the colt's stall.

The half-length victory in the Kentucky Derby was the shortest winning margin of Black Gold's career, but Webb had the colt back under saddle a week later at Maple Heights on the outskirts of Cleveland. Black Gold won the Ohio State Derby in a gallop by three lengths. On July 12 at Hawthorne Park, Black Gold bobbled and went to his knees in the Chicago Derby. Spotting the field nearly twenty lengths going into the first turn, he found his stride and went on to smother the field, winning by eight lengths and becoming the first horse ever to win four Derbies in one season.

Visibly losing flesh, the colt was showing signs of fatigue. A quarter-crack developed in his left fore foot and he was fitted with a bar-shoe. Even though Black Gold could barely walk around the shed row, Webb continued to run him. The colt lost his next two, then won the last race of his three-year-old season at Latonia on September 27. Mooney refused further participation and went to ride in Canada. The campaign was finally over, and Black Gold was retired to stud. As a juvenile and sophomore, Black Gold had a combined record of thirty-one starts, eighteen wins, five seconds, and four thirds, with earnings of $110,503.

The son of Black Toney had fired blazing bullets on the racetrack, but in the breeding shed he shot blanks. After two seasons of futility, Black Gold sired only one foal and lightning killed it. Webb returned Black Gold to training even though the horse was not sound. In pain that was evident to everyone but his trainer, Black Gold ran fifth, fourth, and ninth in his first three starts. So what if Black Gold stepped on a nail? Get him back out on the track. If Black Gold returned to the barn lame, Webb preferred to look at the condition book rather than

## Kentucky Derby
## Purse: $50,000 Added

5th Race Churchill Downs - May 17, 1924. Fiftieth running Kentucky Derby.
Purse $50,000 added. Three-year-olds. 1 1-4 Miles. Main Track. Track: Fast.
Net value to winner, $52,775 and gold trophy; second, $6,000; third, $3,000; fourth, $1,000.

| Horse | A | Wgt | Eqp | Odds | PP | ST | 1/4 | 1/2 | 3/4 | Str | Fin | Jockey |
|---|---|---|---|---|---|---|---|---|---|---|---|---|
| Black Gold | 3 | 126 | w | 1.75 | 1 | 3 | $5^h$ | $6^h$ | $3^x$ | $3^2$ | $1^x$ | J D Mooney |
| Chilhowee | 3 | 126 | w | 15.25 | 13 | 6 | $4^1$ | $3^h$ | $4^{1x}$ | $1^h$ | $2^{no}$ | A Johnson |
| Beau Butler | 3 | 126 | wb | ‡10.25 | 10 | 8 | $15^h$ | $11^{nk}$ | $10^1$ | $10^h$ | $3^h$ | L Lyke |
| Altawood | 3 | 126 | w | 19.10 | 7 | 19 | 19 | $14^1$ | $7^4$ | $5^2$ | $4^h$ | L McDermott |
| Bracadale | 3 | 126 | wb | §3.40 | 12 | 4 | $1^x$ | $1^3$ | $1^2$ | $2^x$ | $5^8$ | E Sande |
| Transmute | 3 | 126 | w | ††10.25 | 2 | 1 | $6^1$ | $4^h$ | $2^2$ | $4^3$ | $6^h$ | L McAtee |
| Revenue Agent | 3 | 126 | w | 26.75 | 5 | 9 | $10^x$ | $8^1$ | $8^h$ | $7^1$ | $7^h$ | D Hurn |
| Thorndale | 3 | 126 | wb | †10.70 | 6 | 11 | $7^1$ | $7^{1x}$ | $5^3$ | $6^x$ | $8^2$ | B Marinelli |
| Klondyke | 3 | 126 | w | †† | 3 | 13 | $8^h$ | $10^h$ | $9^1$ | $9^4$ | $9^4$ | I Parke |
| Mad Play | 3 | 126 | wb | § | 9 | 14 | $11^h$ | $9^x$ | $6^x$ | $8^h$ | $10^x$ | L Fator |
| King Gorin II | 3 | 126 | w | 36.60 | 4 | 12 | $12^2$ | $17^2$ | $12^1$ | $13^1$ | $11^2$ | M Garner |
| Cannon Shot | 3 | 126 | wb | † | 8 | 18 | $18^{1x}$ | 19 | $11^x$ | $12^1$ | $12^{1x}$ | G Ellis |
| Modest | 3 | 126 | ws | † | 16 | 15 | $13^1$ | $18^2$ | $14^h$ | $11^x$ | $13^1$ | J Wallace |
| Diogenes | 3 | 126 | w | † | 15 | 10 | $16^h$ | $15^1$ | $13^1$ | $14^1$ | $14^2$ | C Ponce |
| Nautical | 3 | 126 | w | † | 19 | 7 | $9^h$ | $16^h$ | $15^1$ | $15^h$ | $15^x$ | C Lang |
| Mr. Mutt | 3 | 126 | w | 35.00 | 17 | 17 | $17^1$ | $13^x$ | $17^1$ | $16^1$ | $16^2$ | J Merimee |
| Baffling | 3 | 126 | wb | ‡ | 18 | 2 | $2^x$ | $2^x$ | $16^x$ | $17^h$ | $17^1$ | G W Carroll |
| Wild Aster | 3 | 126 | w | † | 11 | 5 | $3^1$ | $5^1$ | $18^1$ | $18^2$ | $18^4$ | F Coltiletti |
| Bob Tail | 3 | 126 | w | ‡ | 14 | 16 | $14^1$ | $12^x$ | 19 | 19 | 19 | E Blind |

† Mutuel field. ‡ Coupled as Idle Hour Stock Farm Stable entry; § Rancocas Stable entry; †† Harry Payne Whitney entry.

**Off Time:** 4:45  **Time Of Race:** :23⅗  :47⅗  1:13  1:39½  2:05⅖
**Start:** Good and slow  **Track:** Fast
**Equipment:** w for whip; b for blinkers; s for spurs

**Mutuel Payoffs**

| 1 | Black Gold | $5.50 | $5.40 | $4.40 |
|---|---|---|---|---|
| 13 | Chilhowee | | 12.30 | 7.30 |
| 10 | Idle Hour entry | | | 4.70 |

**Winner:** Black Gold, blk. c. by Black Toney—Useeit, by Bonnie Joe (Trained by H. Webb). Bred by Mrs. R. M. Hoots in Kentucky.

**Start good and slow. Won driving; second and third the same.**
BLACK GOLD, well ridden and prominent in the early racing, moved up resolutely after reaching the stretch and disposed of the others in the last 70 yards. CHILHOWEE ran a good race and headed BRACADALE in the last eighth, but tired slightly near the end. BEAU BUTLER closed a great gap and ran an excellent race. ALTAWOOD closed an immense gap after making a slow beginning. BRACADALE tired after leading to the stretch. TRANSMUTE was done after going the first three-quarters. MAD PLAY was always outrun. BAFFLING ran a good three-quarters. The others were never prominent. Scratched—Glide, 121.

**Owners:** (1) Mrs R M Hoots; (2) Gallaher Brothers; (3) Idle Hour Stock Farm Stable; (4) C B Head; (5) Rancocas Stable; (6) H P Whitney; (7) G A Cochran; (8) B Block; (9) H P Whitney; (10) Rancocas Stable; (11) P Coyne; (12) C A Hartwell; (13) E B McLean; (14) Mrs W M Jeffords; (15) J S Cosden; (16) H C Fisher; (17) Idle Hour Stock Farm Stable; (18) Greentree Stable; (19) Idle Hour Stock Farm Stable.
©EQUIBASE

at a swollen knee or a curbed hock. Horsemen turned their heads when Black Gold went to the track. No one wanted to watch the courageous horse hobble back to the barn.

Some horses never try. Some never give up trying. For Black Gold, a thousand furlongs of training and racing were not enough. But one final furlong would prove too much. The end came on January 18,

1928. It was a Wednesday, and Black Gold, then seven years old, was entered in the mile Salome Purse at Fair Grounds. After a poor start Black Gold was shuffled back. He moved up to stalk the pace. Entering the stretch, he passed a few horses, bobbled, and snapped his left fore-leg above the ankle. Despite efforts from his rider to pull him up, Black Gold ran the entire length of the stretch, making it to the finish line on three legs. A farewell to glory. A farewell to pain.

The next day the American flag was lowered to half-mast and public schools in New Orleans closed. Teachers volunteered to take their students to the track on streetcars for Black Gold's burial. As a jazz band played "Auld Lang Syne," a wooden box shrouded in black crepe and containing the hooves and heart of Black Gold was lowered into an infield grave. A group of schoolchildren assembled around the eighth pole came forward and tossed ribbons and bouquets of flowers into the hole in the ground.

Leave it to an old groom to know how to say goodbye. From behind the tote board, carrying a shovel, a black groom in white dress shirt and suspenders began to dig dirt from under the rail. In silence he shoveled the dirt and carried each scoop to the grave. Rich brown dirt. Compositions of clay and sandy loam washed and tumbled down the Mississippi River from the plains and mountain streams of Arkansas, Kentucky, Ohio, maybe even some particles of limestone from the short-grass country of northeast Oklahoma.

*By Gary McMillen*

# The First Lady
## (Regret, 1915)

REGRET WAS THE FIRST FILLY to win the Kentucky Derby, in 1915, and remained the only one for sixty-five years, a distinction that gave her a special place in history. But, in retrospect, this was the lesser of her contributions to racing history. More important than Regret's enduring gender singularity was the boost she gave to the Derby itself. It has been often recorded how her owner, the eastern sportsman and all-around social swell Harry Payne Whitney, was quoted after Regret's 1915 Derby that, "You know, this is the greatest race in America at the present time, and I don't care whether she ever wins a race again. The glory of winning this event is big enough."

That was music, a veritable symphony, to the ears of one Colonel Matt Winn, whom fellow businessmen of Louisville, Kentucky, had convinced thirteen years earlier to abandon his pursuits as a tailor and take on the salvation of a track and a special event.

Churchill Downs and the Kentucky Derby had been born, apparently fully grown, in 1875. Although it was only a few years after the Civil War, Louisville in the 1870s was a thriving river port city of about a hundred thousand people. As a youngster, Colonel Winn had attended the first Derby with his father. Having also witnessed every running since, he was unable to resist the entreaties in 1902 to help save the Derby when it and the track were suffering difficult and perhaps seemingly fatal economic problems.

Some of the problems might have been beyond the control of the track's managers, but some had been the handiwork of those ever-present authors of history — Ego and Greed. Nearly thirty years before a distinguished New York Turfman would pay homage to the race as the greatest in the land, another distinguished racing mogul had dealt it a crippling blow. Ironically, he was a renowned Kentuckian, James Ben Ali Haggin.

Haggin had ventured from his home state to amass a fortune in mining gold, silver, and copper, which permitted him to establish a breeding and racing operation of gargantuan proportions. In addition to his devotion to horses, he was a high roller, and when he came to Louisville with his colt Ben Ali for the 1886 Derby, his intention was to back the colt substantially.

Labor problems — a bane to many a track operator over the decades — disrupted action at Churchill Downs. As recounted in Peter Chew's book *The Kentucky Derby: The First 100 Years*, the track's founder, Colonel M. Lewis Clark, had a run-in with his starter, whose fee he was forced to increase on the spot to keep the fellow and his crew from striking. Then, the firm that leased the betting privileges from the track ownership ran afoul of the bookmakers, who paid individual fees to be allowed to operate. The fee was set at one hundred dollars each, and the bookies banded together to announce they would pay only two thousand dollars in total.

The alternatives to bookmaking at Churchill Downs at the time were pari-mutuel machines, which Clark had imported after seeing them in operation in Paris. However, there were only four of them at the track.

James Ben Ali Haggin planted his name and the name of his horse in Kentucky racing lore simultaneously when Ben Ali won the Derby, but he was perhaps the first owner to win the race and be highly annoyed at the same time. Haggin announced he would ship his entire stable out of Louisville if, by the very next afternoon, track officials had not corrected the inability to bet with bookmakers. A compromise was worked out, and some of the bookmakers returned, but then, as Chew recounted, Haggin got word that "one of the track officials … had asked 'who does Haggin think he is? … to hell with him, anyway.' "

A fellow with private train cars, thousands of acres, scores of hors-

KINETIC CORP.

**Illustration of the first Derby-winning filly**

es, and the money to have just about anything he wants gets used to being treated differently, and Haggin in a huff told his trainer to ship the Haggin horses to New York. Thereafter, Haggin made no secret of his dissatisfaction, and the impression in the East that Churchill Downs and its big race were poor hinterland counterparts to first-class eastern racing was a prevalent notion.

(At least two other principals in Derby victories historically have been presumed to be more annoyed than overjoyed by winning the race. In 1904, as Peter Chew's book retells, trainer C.E. "Boots" Durnell had a disagreement with the owner of Elwood. The owner wanted to run Elwood in the Derby, but Durnell did not. The owner happened to be Durnell's wife. She overruled him and had someone else saddle the horse when her sulky husband refused even to attend the race. Elwood, of course, won.

Likewise, one of the most successful of Derby owners, Colonel E.R.

Bradley, has often been reported as having been highly put out by one of his four Derby victories. Bradley was a gambler as much as a sportsman, and against conventional wisdom about Regret's Derby being the breakthrough to national prominence, he credited the creation of the first Derby winter book in 1917 — with its guaranteed odds available well in advance — as the more pivotal promotion. In 1921 Bradley backed both his entrants, Black Servant and Behave Yourself, but was keen that the former win since he was by the owner's young stallion Black Toney. Alas, Behave Yourself took the prize as jockey Charles Thompson either forgot or was unable to finesse the instructions for a directed verdict. Bradley duly paid the jockey his share of the purse but sacked him at the same time.)

In addition to the trouble Haggin caused, track founder Clark created some of his own problems through his devotion to tradition. He had created the Derby to be a counterpart to England's Epsom Derby, a mile and a half spring test for three-year-olds. While a race of a mile and a half for young horses in England continued to be accepted, American horsemen began to balk at the notion. By 1894 the Louisville *Courier-Journal* praised Clark for his idealism but lamented that racing had become more business than sport and owners were unwilling to pay to enter in the race. The Derby, it quipped, had become "a contest for dogs."

Only thirty-five horses were nominated for the Derby that year, and by the end of the year, a new group replaced Clark's Louisville Jockey Club. The New Louisville Jockey Club spent a hundred thousand dollars on improvements, including a new grandstand, but kept the race distance, and only four horses ran in 1895. In 1896 the distance was reduced to a mile and a quarter, which had begun to reach into the American psyche as "the classic distance" since the success of New York's Suburban Handicap beginning in 1884. The new distance attracted 171 nominations, but in 1897 the coming of a depression stymied any financial progress Churchill Downs and the Derby might have made.

Despite the track's woes, the purse for the Derby was substantial for its day, but, for once, money failed to talk convincingly enough. In 1895 the purse to the winner was $2,970. If the Derby were an event for dogs, the "best in show" still earned slightly more than the winner of New York's vaunted Belmont Stakes. In 1896 Churchill Downs' new organizers upped the purse to six thousand dollars-added, and Mike Dwyer sent his champion Ben Brush down from New York to accept it, but that was the only instance for many years of a major easterner shipping to the Derby. In addition to New York's major racing, Chicago's American Derby had more prestige than the Kentucky event.

By the time Colonel Winn was recruited, the Derby again had languished, its failure perhaps contributing to the mindset of its founder. Clark — ravaged as well by poor health — had taken his own life.

Winn was a large, jovial son of Irish immigrants. Chew described him as "a combination of Irish and southern charm." Winn was said later to have explained his longevity to consuming the best of bourbon and taking visits to French Lick Springs, Indiana, "to recover from the quantities of Estill County ham, roast turkey, beaten biscuits, and other Derby delicacies."

Winn had succeeded as a tailor, and he succeeded as a racetrack impresario, not only in Kentucky but elsewhere. By the end of his life, in 1949 — the year of the Diamond Jubilee of his beloved Derby — Winn was recognized as a masterful manipulator of publicity. He grasped many principles of promotion. One was that, in sports, recognition by the New York media was essential. Brownie Leach, for many years the publicist for Churchill Downs, wrote for *The Blood-Horse* in 1967 that Winn had expressed the strategy, " 'Give me the best five writers in New York on my side and you can have the rest.' His belief in the importance of New York to the Derby accounted for his making that city his headquarters during most of his off-season. If his evenings were not occupied by social engagements, he likely would be in a night spot with the writers or having them visiting his headquarters in the Waldorf Towers."

Author Chew and others blithely assumed that, as the years went on, the presence at the Derby of such major market sports writers as

Damon Runyon, Grantland Rice, Bill Corum, and Red Smith was "on the house," which accounted for their willingness to cover the event. Leach defended his revered boss, but rather meekly, stating that, "Many years ago the colonel was undoubtedly liberal with racing writers in his efforts to get more racing news on sports pages, but that was done more in other locales where he operated racetracks than it was in connection with the Derby."

Leach, of course, was writing from a context of looking back on many years of the Derby's unique popularity as a national event.

**James Rowe**

Whatever Winn's involvement with management of Churchill Downs might have been in his first ten years there, a review of Derby race charts indicates little growth in national prestige from 1902 through 1912. Anti-gambling legislation shut down New York racing in 1911–12, but the major eastern owners tended to look to England as a venue for their best horses rather than sending them to other states still in action.

Then, in 1913, a bit of luck fell Winn's way when Donerail won the Derby and produced a mutuel payoff of $184.90 for two dollars — an event that any sage publicist could use to gain some mileage. The following year brought another boost when Old Rosebud won the Derby in his second start at three. Although he was a virtual house horse, Old Rosebud also owned national status. He had been bred in Kentucky by John E. Madden and raced for Colonel Hamilton C. Applegate, whose family owned a Kentucky distillery, a Thoroughbred farm named Old Rosebud Stock Farm, and a block of shares in Churchill Downs. However, at two, the hardy gelding had won twelve of fourteen starts, concluding with two stakes victories at New York's Saratoga, and he was regarded as the nation's best juvenile.

In addition to the race's attracting the nation's best two-year-old of the previous year, the 1914 Derby Day guest list included August Belmont II, chairman of The Jockey Club and the most prominent Turfman of the time. Old Rosebud had beaten Belmont's brilliant Stromboli in the Flash Stakes at Saratoga, but Belmont had no entrant in the Derby.

The Derby purse, which had remained at $6,000 for most years in Winn's tenure to that time, was upped to $10,000 in 1914, and Old Rosebud netted $9,125. On that occasion the financial timing was in Churchill Downs' favor. Although New York racing had been reinstated in 1913, the purses there were not always what they had been before the interruption. For example, the Futurity, with its lengthy schedule of nomination and eligibility payments, rewarded its winner in 1914 with

R.G. POTTER

**Matt Winn helped popularize the Derby**

$16,010, but its payoff had been as high as $67,675 as early as 1890. The 1914 Belmont Stakes had a first-place purse of $3,025, less than one-third of Old Rosebud's Kentucky Derby purse. Maryland's Preakness was worth only $1,355 to the winner, while the once rich American Derby ($49,500 to the winner in 1893) had not yet been reinstated from its twelve-year hiatus. Kentucky racing was difficult to cast as secondary from a financial standpoint.

At any rate, Harry Payne Whitney allowed his trainer, James Rowe Sr., to point the best juvenile of 1914 toward the Kentucky Derby for her debut at three in 1915.

Whitney's father, William Collins Whitney, had delved into Thoroughbred racing near the end of the nineteenth century, and the son had followed suit. Harry Payne Whitney was the leading owner for the first time in 1914, and he eventually would lead the list five more times. As befits such an outfit, his trainer was one of the great horsemen of the era. In her chapter on the younger Whitney's Regret in the book *Women of the Year* (Eclipse Press, 2004), Avalyn Hunter identified the astounding total of thirty-four champions trained by Rowe. (Champion designations prior to 1936 are unofficial, reflecting a seeming consensus of historians.) In earlier years, Rowe had trained for the dominant James R. Keene stable, which included the unbeaten Colin. Thus, Rowe had the distinction of training one of the few horses to get through a career without defeat as well as the first filly to win the Kentucky Derby. Regret's only jockey at two and three was Joe Notter, who also had ridden Colin.

Regret was a chestnut filly by the outstanding sire Broomstick and out of Jersey Lightning, a daughter of the renowned Hamburg. Jersey Lightning might have been a good name for the filly herself, for Regret was foaled at Brookdale Farm, which Whitney leased near Red Bank, New Jersey.

Jersey Lightning won only one race but was out of Daisy F., a winner of twenty-three races. Daisy F. was by Riley, who was one of the Derby winners of the 1890s that did establish inter-regional credentials, winning the Monmouth Cup, Coney Island Cup, Brooklyn Cup, etc. Daisy F.'s dam was the grand filly Modesty, winner of the 1884 Kentucky Oaks and victor over males in the first American Derby. Jersey Lightning enhanced the strength of this family. In addition to Regret, her five foals included a full brother, Thunderer, who won the Futurity the year his sister won the Derby; Vivid, winner of the Champagne; and another stakes winner, Barnegat.

The juvenile campaign of the lovely, blaze-faced Regret was compacted into fourteen days at Saratoga. Rowe rejected any need of giving her an easy first trial and sent her out against colts in the Saratoga Special. She won by a length from James Butler's Pebbles, who was

NATIONAL MUSEUM OF RACING

**Regret with Whitney (right) and Rowe**

to follow her to — and in — the Derby the next spring. In the Sanford Stakes, Regret carried 127 pounds and defeated Solly by a length and a half. In the Hopeful she survived a traffic shuffle and again defeated Pebbles (third), besting runner-up Andrew M. by a half-length in heavy going. Regret again carried 127 pounds, giving thirteen to the runner-up.

Regret wintered in New Jersey under a training regimen that Rowe had worked out to prep horses for their spring seasons. The late horseman Colonel Phil T. Chinn once said of Rowe's schedule: "On March 1 every year he came out from under the shed at Brookdale. It could be sleeting on March 1, but out he came — and never missed a day of training after that, regardless of the weather. If a horse could withstand his training, you had a race horse. I think maybe he must have slipped

a few big gallops into Regret before March 1 ... she was in beautiful physical condition for the Derby."

Regret and nine other Whitney runners arrived at Churchill Downs on the Sunday before Derby Saturday. It was Rowe's first visit to the track since 1882, when he had trained the Dwyer Brothers' Hindoo, winner of the Louisville Cup. In 1881 he had sent out Hindoo to win the seventh Kentucky Derby.

Under the training philosophy of 1915, Rowe breezed Regret the full Derby route twice in the remaining six days before the race. *The Courier-Journal*'s exultations underscored Winn's success in attracting top horses: "The Churchill Downs course yesterday was alive with lovers of the Turf, drawn there to see the great Eastern horses that have come to the Downs for the spring meeting ... dozens of persons paid a visit to H.P. Whitney's stable to see the great unbeaten filly Regret. They also had the pleasure of seeing the famous daughter of Broomstick

KEENELAND-COOK

**Regret made her first three starts at Saratoga**

under the saddle with the noted jockey Joe Notter up, and she fulfilled every expectation as she moved in regal style around the course."

Pebbles' presence meant that the Derby had not only the top juvenile of the previous year, but also the top two. A field of sixteen went to the post, the largest in the race's history. Under the race's conditions at the time, weights ranged from 110 to 117 pounds, with Regret carrying 112. While no filly had won the race, Lady Navarre had run second in 1906, and, coincidentally, fillies had finished third in each of the last three runnings leading to Regret's effort. All things considered, the crowd made Regret the favorite, but not an overwhelming one, as she went off at slightly more than 5-2. This perhaps reflected rumors that Rowe was on the fence about running her since she was said to be off her feed as a result of her trip from New Jersey.

Notter sent her to the front at the start, and she held sway throughout. Pebbles tried to challenge with five furlongs to run, but Notter let out a notch and Regret turned him back. In the stretch, Pebbles doggedly still pursued her. John O'Connor's *History of the Kentucky Derby (1875–1921)* recorded that "Notter shook up the filly slightly, and she came down the rail two lengths in front of Pebbles ... the unattainable had been attained."

Sharpshooter finished third. Regret's time was 2:05 2/5 on a fast track, two seconds over Old Rosebud's track and stakes record at a mile and a quarter.

Then followed Whitney's glowing pronouncement, which, as recorded the next day in *The Courier-Journal*, ended with the observation, "I have seen much bigger crowds in the East and abroad, but I never saw a more enthusiastic one. It's great."

That he would be extolling his filly and a day of sport is somewhat at odds with what else was happening. Derby Day brought news of the sinking of the *Lusitania* by a German U-boat. Mrs. Whitney's brother, Alfred Vanderbilt, was among those lost, going to his death after giving up his life jacket to a lady. One would assume that Whitney was aware of the disaster but quite likely would not yet have had confirmation that his brother-in-law was among those missing. Later, in the custom of the time, Whitney ceased running horses in his own name for the year, his stock instead racing in the name of a family associate, L.S. Thompson (technically the leading owner of 1915).

While Regret's presence, and victory, produced a first line in a *Courier-Journal* story that "A Filly Has Won the Derby," the article was far off the front page. In New York, the *Times'* three inches of space on the race was less than was allotted notices that Whitney's wife had been appointed to the advisory board of an arts group and that an amateurs' race meeting would be held that day at the Whitneys' estate on Long Island.

The impact of the victory must have been considerable, however. The next year (with no *Lusitania* disaster), the Louisville paper put the Derby on the front page the Sunday after the race and *The New York*

KEENELAND-COOK

*Times*' coverage totaled some twenty-four inches of type.

Winn had the ammunition he needed, and he took full advantage. As his devoted follower Leach wrote, "Col. Winn's personality enabled him to walk with the titans. He numbered among his close friends outstanding men in finance, industry, politics, commerce, and the professions. It was obvious they enjoyed his company and respected his judgment.

"Probably through sheer personality he first persuaded the country's most prominent stables to nominate horses and run them in the Derby … the same magnetic personality drew the country's leading writers, both in and out of sports. Articles by Damon Runyon, Grantland Rice, Irvin S. Cobb, and countless others provided records of that attraction.

"As the importance of the Derby grew, Col. Winn realized that one of his major problems in making it a national event was to attract

**Regret (inside) captures the Hopeful at two over the boys**

more and more people from more distant areas. He approached rail-roads with a suggestion that each take a bloc of good seats and offer them to customers along their respective lines. He offered to take back any tickets not sold by a specific date, that giving him time to dispose of them to waiting customers. The result of that idea was the eventual clogging of every siding in Louisville with special trains from every part of the country, and railroads clamored for larger blocs of tickets. He could not take his show to the people, so he brought the people to his show."

As for Regret, she did moderately well in maintaining the prestige of being the only filly to win the Derby. Historian Walter Vosburgh recorded that Regret caught a cold during her trip to Kentucky. He wondered whether she ever totally recovered from that stress com-bined with the effort of the race itself. As it were, she made no further starts for more than three months, but back at Saratoga she took on The Finn, winner of the Withers Stakes and Belmont Stakes, and left him in the dust as she won the Saranac Handicap at Saratoga by a length and a half. She gave nine pounds to runner-up Trial By Jury.

That was all for Regret at three, but her two victories in two starts gained her after-the-fact designation as best of her age and best of any age in American racing in 1915.

Nearly a year later Regret returned to action, again without a prep, for the one and a quarter-mile Saratoga Handicap. Under 123 pounds, she was giving sixteen pounds of actual weight to the year's top three-year-old colt, Friar Rock, and two pounds to the older male Stromboli while carrying equal weight with 1915's top three-year-old colt, The Finn. The handicap champion Short Grass was top-weight at 132.

Regret set a swift early pace under a pull; then for the first time in her career she weakened. She fell away so severely that she finished last, beaten sixteen lengths by winner Stromboli. Some conjectured she might have been short or not totally recovered from the problem that clouded her status before the Derby. At any rate she was given a more gentle challenge almost three weeks later, winning a one-mile overnight race. Frank Keogh rode her on that occasion. Regret did not run again that year, but Whitney declined to retire her.

The following May she came out under jockey Frank Robinson in an easier spot than in any of her previous seasonal debuts. For the first time in Regret's career, Rowe placed the filly in a race exclusively for her own gender, and it was not a major stakes but a five and a half-furlong allowance. Nonetheless, it was not without its challenges, for she carried 128 pounds, giving ten to Yankee Witch. Regret won by eight lengths.

Next came another plunge into history. The Brooklyn Handicap was renowned for occasioning a meeting of three Kentucky Derby winners. The five-year-old Regret was joined in the field by the 1914 Derby winner Old Rosebud and the current year's (1917) winner, Omar Khayyam. That was not the only difficult part, however, for the field also included the noted handicappers Roamer and Stromboli. Oddly, Regret handled all of these but could not hold off her own stablemate, Borrow.

Borrow had been one of the horses Whitney had sent to England, where the colt won the Middle Park Stakes at two and was regarded as one of the top older males in 1914, but three years later, at the age of nine, he was not reckoned to be still at his best. He carried 117 pounds to Regret's 122. It seems fairly clear that Whitney preferred that Regret win the race.

As usual, Regret tore off in front and seemed to be back at her best as she turned away one challenge after another. In the late going, however, Old Rosebud was persistent, and Willie Knapp, aboard Borrow, might well have thought the stable's success depended on his getting his old guy up to save the day. This is what he did, charging along the inside to win by a nose and setting an American record of 1:49 2/5 for nine furlongs. As it turned out, however, Robinson and Regret turned back Old Rosebud by a length. The damsel had needed no rescue after all.

Whitney was said to have shed tears as he led in his veteran conqueror of his special heroine.

Regret won her two remaining races, the mile and one-sixteenth Gazelle and a seven-furlong handicap, and for the third time in her four years of racing she was regarded as a champion, that time of the older distaff division. This gave her a career mark of nine wins and a second from eleven starts with earnings of $35,093. She never had finished behind another female.

Regret's pride of place in the racing world was enhanced more by the mere passage of years than by her own production record. She had eleven foals, of which six were winners. Her first, Penitent, was stakes placed and foaled the Canadian Coronation Stakes winner Easter Hatter. Regret's next foal, Revenge, won the Yonkers Handicap. This promising start was not followed by additional first-generation success, although Regret's daughters Nemesis and Stigma produced several important steeplechasers for Whitney's son, C.V. Whitney, and Nemesis also foaled flat stakes winners Red Rag and Avenger. Another daughter, Rueful, foaled the most noted of the grandsons in First Fiddle, who won ten stakes and earned $398,610, largely for another owner, Eddie Mulrenan.

Regret died in 1934 and was buried at the Kentucky farm that the Whitney family had established and that was then owned by C.V. Whitney. She was elected to the National Museum of Racing's Hall of Fame in 1957.

Harry Payne Whitney gave concrete evidence of the sincerity of his respect for the Kentucky Derby, starting eighteen additional horses in the race between 1916 and 1927. He won his second Derby in his final attempt: Whiskery took the roses in 1927, when stablemate Bostonian was fifth.

W.C. Whitney had bred the filly Artful, who won the Futurity after his death. Perhaps this early success emboldened the family not to shy from asking fillies to challenge colts. Harry Payne Whitney later won the 1924 Futurity with a filly of his own in Mother Goose and won the 1905 Belmont with Tanya (bred by W.C. Whitney) — still the last filly to win that classic. After Regret, his entrants in the Derby included the high-class filly Prudery, who was coupled with his Tryster as the favored entry in 1921; they finished third and fourth, respectively.

Upon Whitney's death in 1930, son C.V. Whitney took on the stable. The star of that year, the juvenile Equipoise, was injured and

## Kentucky Derby
## Purse: $10,000 Added

**5th Race  Churchill Downs - May 8, 1915. Forty-first running Kentucky Derby.**
Purse $10,000 added. Three-year-olds. 1 1-4 Miles. Main Track. Track: Fast.
Net value to winner, $11,450; second, $2,000; third, $1,000; fourth, $225.

| Horse | A | Wgt | Eqp | Odds | PP | St | 1/4 | 1/2 | 3/4 | Str | Fin | Jockey |
|---|---|---|---|---|---|---|---|---|---|---|---|---|
| Regret | 3 | 112 | w | 2.65 | 2 | 1 | $1^{1x}$ | $1^{x}$ | $1^{x}$ | $1^{1x}$ | $1^{2}$ | J Notter |
| Pebbles | 3 | 117 | wb | 6.55 | 3 | 3 | $2^{1}$ | $2^{1x}$ | $2^{1x}$ | $2^{2}$ | $2^{2}$ | C Borel |
| Sharpshooter | 3 | 114 | wb | 9.60 | 8 | 7 | $3^{x}$ | $3^{x}$ | $3^{h}$ | $3^{1}$ | $3^{1}$ | J Butwell |
| Royal II | 3 | 117 | wb | 15.10 | 10 | 16 | $12^{2}$ | $9^{1}$ | $6^{nk}$ | $5^{h}$ | $4^{3}$ | A Neylon |
| Emerson Cochran | 3 | 117 | w | 16.15 | 5 | 2 | $6^{x}$ | $4^{1}$ | $7^{x}$ | $4^{x}$ | $5^{x}$ | W W Taylor |
| Leo Ray | 3 | 117 | w | 17.90 | 11 | 13 | $10^{h}$ | $8^{1x}$ | $8^{h}$ | $7^{h}$ | $6^{1x}$ | T McTaggart |
| Double Eagle | 3 | 117 | wsb | 17.20 | 13 | 12 | $9^{h}$ | $7^{1x}$ | $9^{x}$ | $6^{2}$ | $7^{4}$ | C Burlingame |
| Dortch | 3 | 110 | w | †5.40 | 1 | 11 | $7^{1}$ | $6^{x}$ | $5^{1x}$ | $8^{x}$ | $8^{5}$ | A Mott |
| For Fair | 3 | 117 | wb | † | 4 | 15 | 16 | 15 | $10^{x}$ | $9^{x}$ | $9^{x}$ | W Warrington |
| Ed Crump | 3 | 117 | wb | ‡5.90 | 7 | 4 | $4^{1x}$ | $5^{x}$ | $4^{x}$ | $10^{x}$ | $10^{h}$ | R Goose |
| Little String | 3 | 117 | w | † | 12 | 10 | $11^{1x}$ | $12^{2}$ | $11^{1}$ | $11^{1}$ | $11^{1x}$ | E Pool |
| Goldcrest Boy | 3 | 114 | w | ‡ | 6 | 8 | $8^{x}$ | $10^{x}$ | $13^{1}$ | $12^{1}$ | $12^{2}$ | J Kederis |
| Uncle Bryn | 3 | 117 | wsb | † | 16 | 14 | $14^{1}$ | $14^{1}$ | $12^{x}$ | $13^{1}$ | $13^{2}$ | J McTaggart |
| Tetan | 3 | 117 | w | §† | 15 | 6 | $13^{2}$ | $13^{2}$ | $14^{6}$ | $14^{6}$ | $14^{2}$ | J Smyth |
| Norse King | 3 | 117 | w | 39.60 | 9 | 9 | $5^{x}$ | $11^{1}$ | $15^{1}$ | $15^{2}$ | $15^{4}$ | W J O'Brien |
| Booker Bill | 3 | 117 | wb | §† | 14 | 5 | $15^{1}$ | 16 | 16 | 16 | 16 | W Andress |

† Mutuel field. ‡ Coupled in betting (J W Schorr entry); § Coupled in betting (Johnson and Crosthwaite-Moore entry).

| **Off Time:** 5:22 | **Time Of Race:** :23¾ | :48¾ | 1:13¾ | 1:39¾ | 2:05¼ |
|---|---|---|---|---|---|

**Start:** Good and slow      **Track:** Fast
**Equipment::** w for whip; b for blinkers; s for spurs

**Mutuel Payoffs**

| 3 | Regret | $7.30 | $4.00 | $3.60 |
|---|---|---|---|---|
| 5 | Pebbles | | 7.60 | 4.80 |
| 11 | Sharpshooter | | | 7.10 |

**Winner:**  Regret, ch. f. by Broomstick—Jersey Lightning, by Hamburg (Trained by James Rowe Sr.).
Bred by H.P. Whitney in New Jersey.

**Start good and slow. Won easily; second and third driving.**
REGRET, from a fast start and well ridden, took the lead at once and was rated in front to the last eighth, where she drew away to win easing up.
PEBBLES raced close up in nearest pursuit all the way and held on gamely in the final drive. SHARPSHOOTER also ran a good race and stood a hard
drive resolutely. ROYAL II closed a big gap from a slow beginning. EMERSON COCHRAN and LEO RAY ran good races. ED CRUMP showed speed but
failed to stay.
Scratched—Kilkenny Boy, 117; Phosphor, 117; Commonada, 117.

**Owners:**  (1) H P Whitney; (2) J Butler; (3) S L Parsons; (4) J Livingston; (5) R L Baker; (6) J T Looney; (7) J F Johnson; (8) W W Darden; (9) G M Miller;
(10) J W Schorr; (11) M B Gruber; (12) J W Schorr; (13) Mrs R W Walden; (14) Johnson & Crosthwaite; (15) F B Lemaire; (16) M C Moore.
©EQUIBASE

could not make the Derby the following year, and another the third-generation Whitney inherited, the grand filly Top Flight, did not contest the race. C.V. Whitney had his own successes with fillies against colts, however, including First Flight's 1946 Futurity score and Bug Brush's world-record performance at one and one-eighth miles in the 1959 San Antonio Handicap. He ran fifteen horses in the Derby without winning, and among the best was the champion filly Silver Spoon, who was fifth in 1959.

As the years passed, Regret's status became more deeply

entrenched in Derby lore, and the Derby, of course, became more entrenched in American sport and culture. It was not until 1980 that another blaze-faced chestnut, Genuine Risk, trod the same path and became the second of her gender to wear the roses. This exclusive girls' club accepted one more member, Winning Colors, in 1988, but no filly has crashed that small circle since.

*By Edward L. Bowen*

# What a Trip!
## (Alysheba, 1987)

WITH ONLY BET TWICE between him and the finish line of the 1987 Kentucky Derby, Alysheba gathered momentum, shifted into high gear, and took aim on the colt only one and a half lengths ahead of him. Standing at the rail at Churchill Downs that afternoon, his groom, John Cherry — a quiet man known as Whispering John — turned to complete strangers next to him and yelled, "Hell, we're going to win it from here!"

But with little more than three-sixteenths of a mile to go, Bet Twice ducked from jockey Craig Perret's whip out into Alysheba's path. Alysheba stumbled, his front legs bending precariously under him. Impending victory turned into impending disaster, as Chris McCarron — only a month returned to the saddle following a horrific spill — envisioned himself and his mount hitting the ground with fifteen horses behind them.

And yet, somehow, Alysheba managed to recover his footing in half a stride and, even more astonishingly, again went after Bet Twice. As Alysheba approached him, Bet Twice swerved out once more, this time forcing Alysheba to alter course around him.

"That probably made him (Alysheba) mad," Cherry said years later, "and you didn't want to make that horse mad."

Alysheba surged past the troublemaking Bet Twice and beat him by three-quarters of a length before 130,532 astounded fans.

"Very few horses would be able to deal with all of that and still go on and win," said McCarron seventeen years later. "He showed the incredible athlete that he was that day."

But while a horse must have athletic ability to win against such obstacles, he also has to be willing.

"This horse gave me every ounce in his body," said Clarence Scharbauer, who bought Alysheba as a yearling and ran him in the name of his wife, Dorothy, and daughter, Pam. "When he'd pin those ears, he meant business."

Alysheba's trainer, Jack Van Berg, put it this way: "He never lied to you. You took him over there, and he was there to win."

The colt brought his honesty, along with a healthy measure of feistiness, to Churchill Downs on Derby Day. Alysheba answered the question of just how good he really was with that single defining moment in the stretch, when he overcame trouble that would have stopped a mere ordinary equine.

However, this powerful, determined colt had only one official win

**Alysheba relies on his courage and heart to capture the roses**

164

in ten starts prior to starting in America's most famous horse race. If he had always wanted to win, how come he had almost always managed to lose? For Alysheba the answer was a combination of his learning to focus his incredible ability and surgery to correct a breathing problem. It all came together on the first Saturday in May and set Alysheba on the path to becoming one of the greatest horses in the final decades of the twentieth century.

But had Preston Madden not answered the telephone one day in late 1973, Alysheba might never have even existed.

Madden bred Alysheba's dam, Bel Sheba, and sold her as a yearling at Keeneland in 1971 to Dr. Ernest Wright for $20,000. She finished third as a two-year-old in the Adirondack Stakes at Saratoga for Wright, but when she had only earned $34,031 by the end of her three-year-old season, he telephoned Madden to ask what he should do with her.

"That's easy," replied Madden, and he promptly traded Wright a Nodouble yearling for the three-year-old.

"My wife, Anita, and I often laugh about it," Madden said, "because if I hadn't been there to take the call, we'd not have been nearly as happy."

Preston Madden had the credentials to breed a Kentucky Derby winner. The Kentuckian's grandfather, John E. Madden, founded the family farm, Hamburg Place, near Lexington and bred five Derby winners on the property — Old Rosebud (who won in 1914), Triple Crown winner Sir Barton (1919, bred in partnership with Vivian Gooch), Paul Jones (1920), Zev (1923), and Flying Ebony (1925). While John Madden didn't breed 1898 winner Plaudit, he did own and train him, giving Madden the unique status of being the only person to have bred, owned, and trained a Derby winner.

Preston Madden never felt pressured by his grandfather's legacy. He and Anita became famous for their fabulous Kentucky Derby parties, but their success in racing ran much deeper. Madden learned his trade well from people such as Hamburg farm manager Jimmy Clyburn, neighbor Owen Campbell, Spendthrift Farm founder Leslie Combs II, Claiborne Farm owner Bull Hancock, and Madden's own study of

number 9

**Alysheba overcomes trouble in the stretch to best Bet Twice and win the roses**

E. MARTIN JESSEE

genetics at the University of Kentucky.

Madden raced grass champion T. V. Lark in the 1960s, and he has been breeding stakes winners for decades.

"I was twenty-seven when we had T. V. Lark," said Madden, still awestruck about his luck forty-plus years later. "My wife and I couldn't believe we could have the champion grass horse. He beat Kelso."

Madden began breeding Thoroughbreds in the mid-1950s and from the beginning couldn't help but feel some sense of destiny.

"From 1955 I was convinced I would breed a Kentucky Derby winner," he said, "but by the time Alysheba came along, I was beginning to be convinced that it would be posthumously."

In 1956 Madden bred his first foal from Blinking Owl, a mare bred by Colonel E.R. Bradley. She had a royal pedigree, being by Pharamond II and out of the Black Servant mare Baba Kenny, but on the track she earned a paltry $1,900. When Bradley died in 1946, Blinking Owl went to the

Greentree Stable of John Hay Whitney and his sister, Joan Whitney Payson, for which she produced six foals, all winners. Madden's step-father, C.F. Morriss, acquired Blinking Owl in 1953, and when he retired from racing two years later, he sold her and several other mares to Madden. Blinking Owl produced three foals in the name of Winifred Morriss, Preston Madden's mother, who co-owned some mares with her son, and the mare earned slight fame for producing at the age of twenty-two Triple Crown winner War Admiral's last foal in 1960. That foal was Belthazar, Alysheba's second dam, bred by Preston Madden.

"I had War Admiral at stud," Madden recalled. "It was very early in

**Alysheba is surrounded by photographers in the winner's circle**

MILT TOBY

my career, and I didn't have many mares."

Because he was eager to get his breeding operation going, Madden didn't break or train Belthazar, preferring to breed her instead of race her.

"I just turned her out and bred her when she was three," he said.

Belthazar produced stakes winner Eager Eagle (by T. V. Lark) and several stakes-placed runners for Madden, three of them fillies by Lt. Stevens. One of the three was Bel Sheba, the filly Madden took back in trade following that opportune telephone call.

By 1983 Bel Sheba had produced two stakes winners, including Port Master, a son of Raise a Native who earned $175,050. Madden explained his decision to breed Bel Sheba to Alydar: "You didn't have to be too enlightened to take her back to the Raise a Native line, and Alydar was the best there was."

Alydar may go down in history as the finest Triple Crown starter never to win a Triple Crown race. Had Affirmed not come along in the 1975 foal crop, Alydar might have won the coveted series. But Alydar brought more than his race record and a budding sire career to Alysheba's pedigree. His Native Dancer top line blended well with the bottom line of War Admiral's sire, the legendary Man o' War, plus two crosses of the fiery Nasrullah in the middle. Throw in 1949 Derby winner Ponder, and Alysheba had the necessary pedigree to win the Run for the Roses.

A commercial breeder, Madden bred Alysheba to sell at the yearling sales, as he did with most of his horses. Two horses he bred had made it to the Kentucky Derby — Vegas Vic in 1971 and Kentuckian in 1972. Madden also owned Kentuckian, who finished tenth in the Derby behind victorious Riva Ridge.

Madden consigned Alysheba to the 1985 Keeneland July yearling sale, where rich Thoroughbred owners from around the world congregated in search of the next superstar. Upper crust East Coast accents mingled with clipped British syllables and exotic Middle Eastern English during inspections at the barn.

Into this scene strode Clarence Scharbauer, a brash cowboy whose family had worked cattle in Texas since 1888. Clarence knew Quarter Horses better than Thoroughbreds, having raised and ridden top-class ranch horses for years as well as having won most of the major Quarter Horse races around the country. In 1975 he had even served as president of the American Quarter Horse Association.

Clarence's father had died in 1942, and his mother and an executor ran the business until Clarence was discharged from the Navy in 1947. From then on Clarence ran several cattle ranches and a sheep ranch, expanding and building upon the business his father and uncle began when they moved from New York to Texas in the late nineteenth century.

Good cattle ranches required good horses, and over the years Clarence developed a rugged band of cowhorses. He understood good horseflesh.

"You've got to know what you're looking for," Scharbauer always said. "Whether it's a Shetland, a Percheron, a Quarter Horse, or a Thoroughbred, get one that's correct."

Scharbauer and his wife, Dorothy, experienced their first Kentucky Derby victory in 1959, when Dorothy's father, Fred Turner, won with Tomy Lee. Clarence and Dorothy had spent many enjoyable afternoons at Ruidoso Downs in New Mexico, which led Clarence to expand his Quarter Horse holdings into the racing side of the breed successfully. But that 1959 Kentucky Derby ultimately brought the Scharbauers to Thoroughbreds.

"After Mr. Turner passed away (in 1965)," Scharbauer said, "my wife said to me for several years she'd really like to go back to the yearling sales at Keeneland and buy two or three horses for four or five years."

Scharbauer assembled a team to take on Keeneland. He hired longtime friend Jay Pumphrey (also a past AQHA president) and Ken Carson, the editor of a southwestern Thoroughbred magazine, to do the pedigree selection and Jack Van Berg to analyze the horses physically and then break and train them. A second-generation Hall of Fame trainer, Van Berg was the son of legendary horseman Marion Van Berg. Jack had led all trainers in the country by number of wins nine times, includ-

E. MARTIN JESSEE

**Pamela, Dorothy, and Clarence Scharbauer and Chris McCarron celebrate**

ing a record 496 wins in 1976, when he also led by purse earnings.

Between Keeneland and the Fasig-Tipton Kentucky sales, the team bought four yearlings. "We got three out of four stakes winners — Alysheba; Exclusive Enough, who won the Hollywood Prevue Stakes; and Stalwart Sal," recalled Carson.

The group initially wanted to buy an attractive son of Mr. Prospector out of the Secretariat mare Secrettame, but at $1.9 million the colt went for too much money. (The Secrettame colt was named Gone West and went on to become a grade I winner and a top sire.) Alydars also were bringing high prices, but Scharbauer team members thought they might get the Bel Sheba colt for a relative bargain because he carried a little less weight than the other youngsters and his full brother, Titanic, wasn't exactly burning up the racetrack for trainer D. Wayne Lukas.

"Alysheba was in his everyday clothes," Van Berg recalled. "He was thin, and I like to buy them that way. It's something I learned from my dad. One of the greater sayings my father always said was, 'Fat is the best color in the world. You take an ugly horse and make him fat and you take a beautiful horse and make him skinny — the ugly one will outsell the skinny one every time.'"

Carson also liked that Alysheba had a few nicks on him. That proved Madden had raised the colt out in a field to be a tough race-horse instead of in a stall so he could look pretty come sale time.

"He just stuck out like a diamond," Van Berg said. "He had a presence about him, like he was the king."

The Scharbauers bought Alysheba for $500,000, a hefty price tag at America's premier sale, but a figure that everyone would later consider a bargain.

Alysheba, whose name combines those of his sire and dam, received his first lessons at Van Berg's farm in Goshen, Kentucky, near Louisville. "When we broke him and would gallop him once around the five-eighths of a mile track, he would be an eighth of a mile in front of everybody else galloping," Van Berg said.

The Scharbauers' yearling purchases were shipped to Van Berg's southern California stable in the spring of their two-year-old season. The trainer soon discovered that Alysheba had not only natural ability but also the intelligence to figure out his daily routine quickly.

Chris McCarron gets his first Derby win

"He was smarter than probably 80 percent of people," Van Berg said. "He knew what he had to do. I'd go out on the racetrack, and he'd stand there for three hours and never pick up a leg. But once he'd gallop, he would not stand. He'd go back to the barn."

To convince Alysheba to exert himself in the mornings, Van Berg usually had to send several of his other runners out against the colt, spacing them at various points in his

172

works. The talented but lazy Alysheba constantly needed a fresh horse to run against or he wouldn't get out of a gallop. Only one horse could do that all by herself — Stalwart Sal, a filly by Stalwart—Delta Sal, by Delta Judge, and another of the Scharbauers' yearling purchases.

As two-year-old racing began in earnest at Hollywood Park, Van Berg entered Stalwart Sal in a maiden race, which she won with such ease that the trainer couldn't resist touting her training partner to his friends on the backstretch.

"You think she can run," he bragged. "You just wait till we run that colt."

The entire Van Berg barn traipsed to the mutuel windows when Alysheba debuted in a five and a half-furlong maiden race at Hollywood on July 21, 1986. Other backstretchers listened to Van Berg and bet their money, sending Alysheba off at 5-2.

"He run fifth — just lollygagged home," Van Berg recalled in disgust.

The trainer took Alysheba on the road with him that summer. The colt lost by a head at Arlington Park in Chicago and then broke his maiden by eight lengths at Turfway Park in northern Kentucky when Van Berg added blinkers. That prompted Van Berg to bump Alysheba into stakes company, where he finished second in Turfway's In Memoriam Stakes (ironically later renamed the Alysheba Stakes and now called the Kentucky Cup Juvenile) and in Keeneland's Breeders' Futurity.

Van Berg knew Alysheba had more ability than the colt was showing in his races, and the losses puzzled him. It wouldn't be until months later when a breathing problem emerged that the trainer would fully understand Alysheba's two-year-old form. "I just thought I didn't have him fit enough for some of them races," Van Berg said with a shrug.

Still, Alysheba had performed well enough to earn a shot in that year's Breeders' Cup Juvenile at Santa Anita. Although Don Brumfield had been riding Alysheba, Dorothy Scharbauer wanted Bill Shoemaker aboard for sentimental reasons. Shoemaker had ridden Tomy Lee for her father in the 1959 Derby.

Alysheba came away from the gate sluggishly, trailing the field early. He managed to make up considerable ground to finish third by two and a half lengths behind eventual Eclipse Award juvenile champion Capote and Qualify, yet two and a quarter lengths in front of fourth-place finisher Bet Twice. Van Berg blamed himself for the result, saying, "I didn't tell Shoe to slap him away from the gate."

The trainer tried Alysheba once more that year, in the $1-million Hollywood Futurity, and Alysheba — this time with Pat Day aboard — lost by a neck to Temperate Sil and the unstoppable team of Charlie Whittingham and Bill Shoemaker. Earlier that year, seventy-three-year-old Whittingham and fifty-four-year-old Shoemaker had combined to win the Kentucky Derby with Ferdinand, a horse Alysheba later faced several times.

Van Berg gave Alysheba three months off between the colt's two- and three-year-old seasons but kept him at the racetrack. For sixty days Van Berg put a rider up just to walk Alysheba in the shed row.

If Van Berg thought Alysheba would impress the trainer's cronies in his racing debut, the trainer expected even more from the colt in his first race at three. Despite his stakes placings Alysheba was still eligible for a non-winners of two in March of 1987 at Santa Anita. Pat Day flew in from the Midwest to ride the odds-on favorite.

Alysheba turned in one of the most disappointing races of his career. He finished a lackluster fourth, losing by five lengths.

"I wanted to jump off the grandstand," Van Berg said. "That was worse than the first start of his life. He just galloped around."

Veterinarian Scott Merrell suspected more than laziness. He suggested scoping Alysheba, and he diagnosed an entrapped epiglottis, which required surgery. The epiglottis, a triangular flap of skin connected to the base of the trachea, can partially block a horse's airway if it becomes entrapped.

Merrell wanted to try a new standing procedure on Alysheba that wouldn't require as much recovery time. "With the standard surgery," Merrell said, "if we'd cut open the throat, he wouldn't have been able to run in any of the Triple Crown races."

The vet first had to convince Van Berg.

"Jack's a pretty stubborn guy," Merrell said. "I knew Jack pretty well, and I knew that the best way to get him to do the surgery was to challenge him."

One day Merrell's truck broke down, and Van Berg, who was headed out of town, gave him a ride to the airport. Merrell spent the entire journey pleading his case.

"I told him he could play it safe and if he ended up losing he'd regret it all of his life," said Merrell. "I said it's a rare guy who has the guts to take a chance. This was a once-in-a-lifetime opportunity, and this surgery was the only way the horse could make the Kentucky Derby."

Van Berg entered Alysheba in the San Felipe Handicap, a major prep for the Santa Anita Derby, wanting to wait for one more race before deciding about surgery. This time Alysheba finished second to Chart the Stars, who never won another stakes. Day told Van Berg that the trainer's colt didn't have the will to win and opted to ride Arkansas sensation Demons Begone in the Kentucky Derby. Van Berg, after getting approval from the Scharbauers, told Merrell to perform the new procedure.

What was supposed to last about five minutes after prepping turned into a tense three hours for Merrell.

"Alysheba was the kind of horse that you had to let do his own thing," Merrell said. "He wanted to play the tough guy for about five minutes, and then usually you could do what you needed to do. Well, that day it took about two and a half hours just to get him prepped for the procedure. He was really fighting me."

Merrell had to insert an endoscope in Alysheba's right nostril to look at the entrapped area, apply a local anesthetic, and then insert a hook-shaped surgical blade into the left nostril to cut the membrane down the middle and free the epiglottis. Merrell just needed a three- to five-minute window of opportunity, which Alysheba didn't want to give him.

"What Alysheba kept doing was flipping his soft palate over where I had to do the operation," Merrell said. "He finally settled down, and I got in and got it done."

The surgery caused Alysheba to miss the Santa Anita Derby, so Van

Berg pointed him for the Blue Grass Stakes at Keeneland in Kentucky. It would be Alysheba's first partnership with Chris McCarron, who would ride him for the rest of his career.

McCarron was recovering from a bad spill the previous fall in a race at Santa Anita. His mount, Variety Road, and three other horses fell over Encolure, who broke down near the three-eighths pole and had to be destroyed. It was one of the worst accidents in Santa Anita history. It ended jockey Terry Lipham's career, and McCarron didn't ride until the following March.

"I didn't fully expect to get on a real live (Kentucky Derby) mount at such a late time," McCarron said, "being not necessarily as fit as I could be and all of the other things that you've got to go through to come back as far as building business."

Fortunately for McCarron, Van Berg had already given him the call on Alysheba before the horse was ready to work for the first time following the throat surgery. Otherwise, Gary Stevens might have ended up riding the colt.

"Gary worked him five-eighths of a mile," Van Berg said, "and when he came back, he said, 'Jack, this is one of the only horses I ever rode that when I chirped at him at the quarter pole, he threw me behind the saddle. I'll sign a contract with you to ride that horse anywhere he goes.' Gary was very impressed."

The Blue Grass Stakes is an excellent barometer of Derby-worthy horses. Spectacular Bid, Riva Ridge, Northern Dancer, and Tomy Lee are among those who won it prior to their Derby victories.

Alysheba successfully used the race, too, and finished first by a head, but his victory was not allowed to stand. Down the stretch he jumped the starting-gate tracks, bumping the LeRoy Jolley-trained Leo Castelli in the process. The stewards disqualified Alysheba to third, moving D. Wayne Lukas-trained War into first and Leo Castelli into second.

"When he jumped, he altered course slightly," McCarron said. "He went out and bumped Leo Castelli a little bit. It's a shame because he was the best horse."

Despite the disqualification, Alysheba demonstrated his ability to

**Alysheba (center) wins the Blue Grass Stakes but is disqualified to third**

McCarron that day. And this performance in his first race following the surgery explained his earlier form to Van Berg, who had known the colt had great ability from his earliest training days.

A large field loomed for the 1987 Kentucky Derby, primarily because a different horse seemed to win every prep race around the country. In addition, one of the favorites, Demons Begone, was prepping in Arkansas, a path few horsemen believed appropriate for winning the Derby. Only Sunny's Halo in 1983 had won the Arkansas Derby and the Kentucky Derby, and he had wintered in southern California. (It wasn't until twenty-one years later that Smarty Jones put those two races together, earning a $5-million bonus for winning the Rebel Stakes and Arkansas Derby at Oaklawn Park and then the Kentucky Derby.)

In 1987 Demons Begone started his campaign by capturing the Southwest Stakes before adding the Rebel and the Arkansas Derby. Arkansas resident John Ed Anthony raced Demons Begone in his Loblolly Stable colors, the same ones Temperence Hill sported seven years earlier when he won the Rebel, Arkansas Derby, Belmont Stakes, Travers Stakes, Jockey Club Gold Cup, and Super Derby.

Temperate Sil, the Whittingham trainee who had defeated Alysheba in the Hollywood Futurity, was a son of Temperence Hill. Temperate Sil came to Kentucky as the Santa Anita Derby winner with a huge chance to give Whittingham back-to-back Derby wins. But the weekend before the big race, a virus and high fever knocked Temperate Sil out of the race.

"I respected Charlie," Van Berg said. "He was a dear friend of mine. He had as much class and was as good a horseman as ever was on the racetrack. So when his horse got sick, I felt bad for Charlie, although he did beat me a God-darn nose in the Hollywood Futurity for a million dollars. I said, 'Charlie, you ain't got nothing to do. Why don't you just stay with me this week?' So he did. He walked to the track with me and back, and we told stories and joked all week."

Whittingham knew the calm attitude a horse needed to survive the craziness of Derby week, and he saw it in Alysheba, who never turned a hair or lathered up despite all the commotion. Whittingham made a comment to Van Berg that the trainer has always remembered.

"We were walking to the track one morning, and Charlie said, 'Jack, this horse has got the best nervous system. You could take a handful of flour and throw it between his hind legs and none of it would stick.'"

The pressure of Derby week never did bother Alysheba. Van Berg would accompany Alysheba and assistant Joe Petalino, who galloped the colt, to the track. Alysheba enjoyed watching everyone else's training moves before stepping out for his own morning exercise.

Seventeen horses entered the 113th Kentucky Derby, a group that impressed Van Berg then and now. He recalled that Alysheba's rivals made more money during their careers than perhaps any group of Derby runners up to that time.

Three in the field — Fountain of Youth winner Bet Twice, Florida Derby winner Cryptoclearance, and Wood Memorial winner Gulch — ultimately earned more than three million dollars each. When the 1987 Derby runners had all finished racing, Alysheba's sixteen rivals together had banked $16,456,655.

A field of seventeen meant traffic, and that year it wasn't confined to Alysheba's stretch trouble.

"Everyone remembers the incident at the head of the stretch vividly," McCarron said. "But the start also was very rough. Alysheba broke a little bit slow, and about fifty yards out of the gate and continuing on for about a sixteenth of a mile, I was getting slammed. I finally had to snatch up and that put me much farther back than I wanted to be in a large field like that."

On the Line and Capote, two of the three-horse Lukas-trained entry, battled each other for the lead, while right behind them a major traffic jam was developing.

"Going around the first turn, about thirty to forty yards in front of me it looked like someone was going to go down," McCarron said, "because Masterful Advocate was crowding a lot of horses down inside of him. There were a lot of horses that were in a space where there was only room for a few. It was a very rough-run first turn, and I was just back there praying that nobody falls."

Nobody did, though immediately after the race jockey Jose Santos blamed the jostling for the blood all over Cryptoclearance. Santos thought his horse had cut his shoulder, but it turned out to be blood from the favorite, Demons Begone.

Rounding the first turn, Demons Begone showed little to Pat Day. The jockey tried to get his colt into the race — after all, they only had one chance at the Kentucky Derby — but he soon realized that something was seriously wrong.

"I had already begun to ease him when I looked down and saw blood coming from his nostrils," Day said.

The colt's vet, Gary Lavin, watched with binoculars from the grandstand. Before the field had gone a half-mile, Lavin had put down his glasses and headed for the stricken favorite.

Demons Begone had bled profusely from his nose. He had never bled before and wasn't running on anti-bleeder medication. The colt recovered to race later that year and at four, but he was never the same.

While Day was pulling up Demons Begone, McCarron was moving Alysheba to the outside going into the backstretch to keep the dirt out of his mount's face. Once Alysheba found room, he began to advance quickly, and McCarron had him in high gear leaving the three-eighths pole.

Then Bet Twice veered out, and Alysheba nearly dropped to his knees.

Assistant trainer Joe Petalino stood in the tunnel at track level and couldn't see the horses, so he watched the network coverage on a nearby television. "When he went down, I thought, 'Well, that's the end of that.' But he gets up. Then he gets bothered again, and I said, 'Now we're really done.'"

Despite Bet Twice's antics, Alysheba powered down the stretch to win in 2:03 2/5, well off Secretariat's Derby record of 1:59 2/5. When the press criticized the time, Van Berg retorted with perhaps his most famous remark about the race: "Time counts only in prison."

The press also quickly credited McCarron with picking Alysheba up so that the colt could recover his footing and win. The jockey modestly declined credit, pointing out that it is impossible for a 112-pound rider to "pick up" a thousand-pound racehorse.

"What you need to do is maintain your balance as best you can and get out of their way when they're trying to rebalance," McCarron said. "You can react in such a way that you're going to help them recover, and conversely you can get in their way and cause them not to recover. So I'll take credit for that, but I won't take credit for picking him up."

Alysheba gave everybody on his team a first Kentucky Derby victory: the Scharbauers as owners, Van Berg as trainer, McCarron as jockey, and Madden as breeder. Madden recalled a special favor that Clarence Scharbauer did for him.

"Clarence had his entire family there," Madden said. "They were all standing up on that rise with the governor, and Clarence did the nicest thing. He said, 'Where's Preston Madden? Preston, get up here.' I said I couldn't. He said, 'Bring Anita. Both of you get up here.' I don't know if he even realized what he did for me. That is the most enviable place

## Kentucky Derby
## Purse: $350,000 Added

**8th Race Churchill Downs - May 2, 1987. 113th running Kentucky Derby.**
**Purse $350,000 added. Three-year-olds. 1 1-4 Miles. Main Track. Track: Fast.**
**Value of race $793,600. Net value to winner, $618,600 and gold trophy; second, $100,000; third, $50,000; fourth, $25,000.**

| Horse | A | Wgt | Eqp | Odds | PP | 1/4 | 1/2 | 3/4 | 1 | Str | Fin | Jockey |
|---|---|---|---|---|---|---|---|---|---|---|---|---|
| Alysheba | 3 | 126 | b | 8.40 | 3 | $14^{2}$ | $13^{2\frac{1}{2}}$ | $7^{\frac{1}{2}}$ | $3^{1}$ | $2^{1\frac{1}{2}}$ | $1^{\frac{3}{4}}$ | C J McCarron |
| Bet Twice | 3 | 126 | | 10.10 | 14 | $5^{\frac{1}{2}}$ | $6^{1}$ | $4^{1}$ | $1^{h}$ | $1^{1}$ | $2^{2\frac{3}{4}}$ | C Perret |
| Avies Copy | 3 | 126 | b | f-24.50 | 16 | $10^{h}$ | $10^{2}$ | $8^{\frac{1}{2}}$ | $4^{h}$ | $3^{1}$ | $3^{nk}$ | M Solomone |
| Cryptoclearance | 3 | 126 | | 6.50 | 1 | $16^{1\frac{1}{2}}$ | $15^{1\frac{1}{2}}$ | $14^{\frac{1}{2}}$ | $7^{\frac{1}{2}}$ | $4^{\frac{1}{2}}$ | $4^{\frac{1}{2}}$ | J A Santos |
| Templar Hill | 3 | 126 | b | f-24.50 | 4 | $9^{h}$ | $11^{1\frac{1}{2}}$ | $9^{2}$ | $9^{\frac{1}{2}}$ | $6^{\frac{1}{2}}$ | $5^{\frac{1}{2}}$ | G W Hutton |
| Gulch | 3 | 126 | | b-4.90 | 6 | $15^{1\frac{1}{2}}$ | $16^{h}$ | $15^{\frac{1}{2}}$ | $12^{1}$ | $7^{3}$ | $6^{\frac{1}{2}}$ | W Shoemaker |
| Leo Castelli | 3 | 126 | b | b-4.90 | 8 | $7^{h}$ | $4^{\frac{1}{2}}$ | $5^{1}$ | $6^{1}$ | $5^{1\frac{1}{2}}$ | $7^{5}$ | J Vasquez |
| Candi's Gold | 3 | 126 | | 48.50 | 12 | $3^{\frac{1}{2}}$ | $3^{h}$ | $6^{1\frac{1}{2}}$ | $8^{h}$ | $8^{2\frac{1}{2}}$ | $8^{2\frac{3}{4}}$ | S Hawley |
| Conquistarose | 3 | 126 | b | 52.80 | 15 | 17 | 17 | 16 | 16 | $13^{4}$ | $9^{2}$ | J D Bailey |
| On The Line | 3 | 126 | b | a-6.30 | 9 | $1^{\frac{1}{2}}$ | $2^{2\frac{1}{2}}$ | $1^{\frac{1}{2}}$ | $2^{1\frac{1}{2}}$ | $9^{\frac{1}{2}}$ | $10^{2}$ | G L Stevens |
| Shawklit Won | 3 | 126 | b | 50.20 | 13 | $11^{\frac{1}{2}}$ | $9^{\frac{1}{2}}$ | $11^{1}$ | $11^{\frac{1}{2}}$ | $12^{\frac{1}{2}}$ | $11^{nk}$ | R Migliore |
| Masterful Advocate | 3 | 126 | | 6.20 | 7 | $6^{h}$ | $7^{\frac{1}{2}}$ | $10^{\frac{1}{2}}$ | $13^{\frac{1}{2}}$ | $11^{\frac{1}{2}}$ | $12^{no}$ | L Pincay Jr |
| War | 3 | 126 | b | a-6.30 | 2 | $8^{1\frac{1}{2}}$ | $5^{\frac{1}{2}}$ | $3^{\frac{1}{2}}$ | $5^{\frac{1}{2}}$ | $10^{1}$ | $13^{7}$ | W H McCauley |
| Momentus | 3 | 126 | b | f-24.50 | 11 | $12^{1\frac{1}{2}}$ | $12^{1}$ | $13^{2}$ | $15^{3}$ | $14^{3}$ | $14^{2\frac{1}{2}}$ | D Brumfield |
| No More Flowers | 3 | 126 | | 55.30 | 17 | $4^{1\frac{1}{2}}$ | $8^{\frac{1}{2}}$ | $12^{2}$ | $14^{2}$ | $15^{1\frac{1}{2}}$ | 15 | W A Guerra |
| Capote | 3 | 126 | | a-6.30 | 5 | $2^{2\frac{1}{2}}$ | $1^{1\frac{1}{2}}$ | $2^{h}$ | $10^{1}$ | 16 | — | A Cordero Jr |
| Demons Begone | 3 | 126 | | 2.20 | 10 | $13^{1}$ | $14^{1\frac{1}{2}}$ | — | — | — | — | P Day |

Capote, Eased; Demons Begone, Bled.

Coupled: a-On The Line, War, and Capote; b-Gulch and Leo Castelli.

f-Mutuel field.

**Off Time:** 5:35 **Time Of Race:** :22⅘ :46⅖ 1:11 1:36⅘ 2:03⅖
**Start:** Good For All **Track:** Fast
**Equipment:** b for blinkers

**Mutuel Payoffs**

| | | | | |
|---|---|---|---|---|
| **4** | **Alysheba** | **$18.80** | **$8.00** | **$6.20** |
| **9** | **Bet Twice** | | **10.00** | **7.20** |
| **14** | **Avies Copy** | | | **6.80** |

**Winner:** Alysheba, b. c. by Alydar—Bel Sheba, by Lt. Stevens (Trained by Jack C. Van Berg). Bred by Preston Madden in Ky.

**Start good. Won driving.**

ALYSHEBA, carefully handled when caught in close quarters between horses just after the start, advanced steadily to reach contention approaching the stretch, stumbled when he clipped the heels of BET TWICE just inside the final three-sixteenths, came out to avoid that rival again leaving the furlong grounds and proved best under strong handling. BET TWICE, never far back, rallied from the outside approaching the end of the backstretch, caught ON THE LINE soon after starting the final turn, then swerved repeatedly under pressure during the drive bothering ALYSHEBA a couple of times and continued on gamely. AVIES COPY moved within easy striking distance from the outside nearing the far turn, remained a factor to midstretch and finished with good energy. CRYPTOCLEARANCE lacked room along the inside after the start, moved fast from the outside leaving the far turn but wasn't good enough. TEMPLAR HILL rallied approaching the stretch and was going well at the finish. GULCH, eased back between horses soon after the start, raced very wide into the stretch but failed to seriously menace with a mild late response. LEO CASTELLI, caught in tight quarters between horses racing into the first turn, moved up along the inside entering the backstretch, raced within easy striking distance to the upper stretch but lacked the needed response. CANDI'S GOLD raced forwardly until near the stretch and tired. CONQUISTAROSE was without speed. ON THE LINE raced outside CAPOTE while vying for the lead, held on well for a mile and flattened out. SHAWKLIT WON tired. MASTERFUL ADVOCATE, caught in close quarters racing into the first turn, was finished before reaching the far turn. WAR lacked room between horses following the start and again along the inside at the first turn, continued to save ground while making a run approaching the end of the backstretch but was finished after going a mile. MOMENTUS failed to be a serious factor. NO MORE FLOWERS showed some early foot while racing wide. CAPOTE raced well from the rail while vying for the lead to the far turn, gave way suddenly, and was eased through the final 70 yards. DEMONS BEGONE, outrun early, bled after entering the backstretch.

**Owners:** (1) Dorothy & Pamela Scharbauer; (2) Cisley Stable & Blanche P Levy; (3) T B Badgett; (4) P Teinowitz; (5) E J Kowitz; (6) P M Brant; (7) P M Brant; (8) Royal Lines (lessee); (9) H DeKwiatkowski; (10) E V Klein; (11) E Anchel; (12) Belles (lessee) & Leveton; (13) T Gentry; (14) Duckett & Winchell, et al.; (15) A I Appleton; (16) Beal & French & Klein; (17) Loblolly Stable



on the planet to be — on that rise after the Kentucky Derby. He could have asked any number of people to join him, but no one else would it have meant more to."

Alysheba had found his stride at the right time, and two weeks later he added the Preakness, standing poised to become racing's twelfth Triple Crown winner. And though Bet Twice thwarted Alysheba's bid in the Belmont (where the Scharbauer runner finished fourth), Alysheba still had victories against 1986 Derby winner Ferdinand, a Breeders' Cup Classic triumph, and a Horse of the Year title in his future. In fact, the two Derby winners, Alysheba and Ferdinand, would square off four times, with Alysheba beating his older foe three out of four.

When Alysheba retired at the end of 1988, he had earned $6,679,242, more than any other horse in North American racing history. And he retired sound. "The day that he retired he was as sound as the day he was born," Van Berg said seventeen years later at Santa Anita.

As Van Berg reminisced, another Derby-winning trainer, Bob Baffert, stopped to listen. After the two swapped a few good-natured insults, Baffert thought back to Alysheba's Derby. "He fell down and came up and won," Baffert said. "It was awesome. If you had waited (to retire him) until he was five years old, they'd have never beat him."

Clarence Scharbauer voiced those same sentiments halfway across the country, at Lone Star Park, when he and Dorothy took part in the unveiling of a larger-than-life-sized bronze of their champion a few weeks before the 2004 Breeders' Cup was held at the Texas track.

"He'd just lope like a deer," said Clarence with tears in his eyes. "He was something special. We should have gone on and run him as a five- or six-year-old. Jack wanted to."

Alysheba retired to William S. Farish III's Lane's End Farm in Kentucky. He failed to duplicate himself as a sire and in 2000 went to stud in Saudi Arabia. While that may have taken him away from his American fans, his Derby stretch run remains an indelible picture.

"Willard Proctor probably described it best," said Van Berg, "and I think Willard Proctor was as good a horseman as ever lived. He told me later, 'Jack, most horses when they go a mile and a quarter they're looking for somewhere to lay down at the eighth pole. This horse got down and got back up and still beat them. That's a helluva horse.'"

*By Tracy Gantz*

# Mr. Longtail
## (Whirlaway, 1941)

WHIRLAWAY HAD EVERY RIGHT to be a good horse on pedigree. Yet the same bloodlines that promised great physical talent were also cursed with defects of temperament and mind, which Whirlaway inherited in full measure. Eccentric to a fault, Whirlaway would never have plumbed his remarkable potential in the hands of an average trainer. It took training as exceptional as the horse himself to tap the colt's tremendous ability and bring him to the edge of greatness.

His dam, Dustwhirl, never raced, but she had already produced the good stakes winner Reaping Reward. She was by Belmont Stakes winner and two-time leading broodmare sire Sweep — also the maternal grandfather of 1937 Triple Crown winner War Admiral — out of the stakes-winning race mare Ormonda, whose fine sons Osmand and Brevity had run second in the 1927 and 1936 Kentucky Derbies, respectively. The female family had already produced one Kentucky Derby winner in Bubbling Over, the 1926 victor, and would later be responsible for the crack handicap mare Honeymoon, 1982 Horse of the Year Conquistador Cielo, and French Classic winner Ta Rib.

Blenheim II, the sire of Whirlaway, had been an excellent racehorse in England, where he won the 1930 Epsom Derby. He stood in France for six seasons beginning in 1931 and was then exported to the United States at a price of 45,000 pounds.

By that time, Blenheim II had already sired the 1936 Epsom Derby winner Mahmoud and the 1937 Italian champion three-year-old Donatello II, both of whom later became important sires, and one might well wonder why the Aga Khan chose to sell a successful stallion at the height of his powers. Most observers believed it was due to the increasing political tensions in Europe, but Jimmy Jones, the younger of the famous father-and-son training team at Calumet Farm, had another explanation.

"He got so many crazy colts," Jones said. "Those English trainers didn't want to fool with them."

Whirlaway was from Blenheim II's first American-sired crop, and he certainly helped establish his sire's reputation in the United States for getting both quality and high-strung temperaments — not to mention possible mental impairment. Ben A. Jones, father of Jimmy Jones and the senior trainer at Calumet, bluntly called Whirlaway "the dumbest horse I ever trained." (Sportswriter Bill Corum made the same point a little more diplomatically when he said of Whirlaway that "you could teach him, but you couldn't teach him much.") Jimmy Jones, equally blunt, called Whirlaway "a nut."

Not only was Whirlaway less than bright, but he also was highly strung. If not quite in the same class of nerves as the similarly sired

**The high-strung Whirlaway escorted by Pinky Brown on the lead pony**

Saratoga, who literally trembled and dripped sweat every time he went to the paddock, Whirlaway was still, in Jones' words, "as nervous as a long-tailed cat in a room full of rocking chairs." He wasn't mean, but between his nervous disposition and his limited intellect, it took a lot of time and patience to get him used to the most routine parts of a racehorse's life — the starting gate, the saddling paddock, the sight of other horses galloping at the track.

There was no question that Whirlaway had talent. In his debut at Chicago's now-defunct Lincoln Fields track at two, he bolted for the outside rail at the start, followed it all the way around the track, and still won. He turned in a similar performance in his first stakes win, the Saratoga Special. In that race he nearly fell at the start and then bolted for the outer rail coming into the final turn despite the best efforts of Hall of Fame jockey Johnny Longden. Last into the home-stretch and once again running on the extreme outside — he actually hit the rail at one point — he once again found enough to win.

But although he won four stakes (and seven of sixteen starts overall) as a juvenile, Whirlaway's erratic running style cost him several races, including the rich Pimlico Futurity. The crowds loved the excitement the Calumet colt brought into a race, making him a great fan favorite before the end of his two-year-old season, but the colt's behavior was more headache than thrill for his trainer. Despite Ben Jones' assigning himself as the colt's personal tutor while Jimmy handled the rest of the Calumet string, Whirlaway continued to lag at the start and bear out. Blinkers, which the colt started wearing midway through his juvenile season, did not help much. To add to his sins, if he made the lead early, he sometimes tried to pull himself up or started wandering erratically all over the track, apparently bored with his solitude. The exasperated senior Jones openly referred to the colt as the "half-wit" and a "knucklehead."

In calmer moments Jones theorized that when Whirlaway got out toward the middle of the track, he literally got lost. He couldn't see the rail to orient himself, and once his mental processes got fogged, that was when the crazy behavior started. When he reached the outer rail,

KINETIC CORP.

Whirlaway romps to an eight-length
victory in the Kentucky Derby

Mr. Longtail

he finally had a point of reference, but, of course, by that time he had lost a tremendous amount of ground — especially since he typically insisted on staying there for the rest of the race. Why not? From Whirlaway's point of view, he had something to tell him where he was, and there weren't any other horses around to force him away from it and leave him lost again.

Through patient observation Jones found that the only thing the colt responded well to was a strict routine with absolutely no deviations; even something so simple as asking the colt to take an alternate route to the track in the morning could result in an equine tantrum. Because Whirlaway was essentially a one-run horse who could not easily regroup if his burst of speed was interrupted in any way, Jones also decided to leave the colt's tail long and uncut, figuring that the whipping, waving mass of horsehair would keep other animals from running up on the colt's heels and perhaps keep them from throwing him off stride. As a result, while most Thoroughbreds had tails ending just below their hocks, Whirlaway's nearly brushed the ground, earning him the nicknames "Mr. Longtail" and "The Flying Tail."

Trying to calm Whirlaway's nerves during the winter following the colt's juvenile season, Jones spent endless hours grazing the colt on a lead shank in the infield of the Calumet Farm training track, letting him watch as other horses worked out. The veteran trainer walked him around the paddocks and let the colt sniff and inspect the starting gate to his heart's content.

Jones' efforts improved Whirlaway's manners, but the colt remained thoroughly unpredictable as a runner. With almost any other horse, Jones would have either thrown in the towel or at least demanded that the gelding knife be applied, but Whirlaway was far and away his best prospect for the 1941 Kentucky Derby. He had speed and as much stamina as any of the other two-year-olds had been asked to show, and he had demonstrated real courage in winning the Hopeful Stakes despite an eye injury that put him on the shelf for nearly a month. The co-champion two-year-old male of 1940 with Futurity Stakes winner Our Boots, Whirlaway led the

Experimental Free Handicap. He also led the juvenile division of 1940 with earnings of $77,275 for the year but could have had much more had he been more manageable.

Coming off a hard juvenile campaign that had ended in mid-November of 1940, Whirlaway resumed training at Hialeah in early 1941. He won his seasonal debut on February 8 in a six-furlong allowance race and then ran third in a similar event ten days later. At that point Calumet owner Warren Wright began pressuring Jones to enter the colt in the Flamingo Stakes, Hialeah's premier race for three-year-olds and an event that Wright wanted very much to win. Jones, however, felt the colt needed more rest and did not want to jeopardize Whirlaway's Kentucky Derby preparation by running him too hard and too soon for a lesser prize.

THE BLOODHORSE

**Eddie Arcaro**

Wright, a hard-headed and astute businessman but not an experienced horseman, was not one to be easily told "no" by any employee. He was used to having a hand in almost every aspect of Calumet's operations and had already fired Frank Kearns, the trainer before Jones, for not perform-ing up to expectations. Further, he knew that his colt would be facing unheralded opponents and could very well win even if not in his best form. Unable to get Wright to agree with the trainer's impression of the colt's needs, Jones reached back into his bag of tricks for a solution.

Jones had once trained at the old Juarez racetrack in Mexico at a time when Mexican bandit and revolutionary hero Pancho Villa was the unofficial power in the area. On one occasion Jones got the word that Villa's men were coming down the shed row and taking all the black horses, apparently for some sort of honor guard. Jones' best horse, a colt named Lemon Joe, was black. Thinking fast, Jones quick-ly applied a heavy coating of mud to one of Lemon Joe's forelegs —

including a ball of mud shoved into the hoof itself — and then put on a heavy bandage. When Villa's men got to Lemon Joe's stall, they found the colt hobbling around and looking the very picture of a bad-legged racehorse. They led him out, circled him around once, and put him right back in his stall. After they were safely gone, Jones undid the bandages, hosed off the mud, and Lemon Joe was as good as new.

Apparently remembering the Lemon Joe incident, Jones set about doing something similar with Whirlaway. He applied a light blister to one of Whirlaway's legs, bandaged him up, and started moaning to all and sundry about the colt's lameness. Wright, seeing the horse done up in bandages, assumed the story was true and dropped his insistence that Whirly run in the Flamingo. Jones smiled to himself, and Whirlaway got his rest.

A few weeks later Wright threatened to become a problem again. Coming off nearly five weeks' rest, Whirlaway had run a dull third in an allowance at Tropical Park. Jones, sensing that his star needed a good tightener to sharpen his speed, dropped Whirlaway's name into the entry box for a five and a half-furlong sprint at Tropical Park a few days after the loss. Wright, who was away fishing in the Florida Keys, saw the colt's name in the entries when reading the morning's *Miami Herald* and rushed back to Tropical Park. In an eyeball-to-eyeball confrontation with his trainer, Wright demanded to know why a stayer was being put in a sprint race and insisted that the colt be withdrawn. Jones, equally furious, informed Wright that he was the trainer and darned well knew what he was doing. Whirlaway ran, getting up in the last stride to win, and Wright cooled down as he accepted his friends' and acquaintances' congratulations. He later apologized, promising to leave the horse training to Jones from there on out.

That solved the owner problem, but it didn't solve the problem of Whirlaway's racing style, which was more erratic than ever. He won an overnight race at Keeneland on April 11 with no problems, but in the Blue Grass Stakes, at the same track, he bore out badly and was beaten six lengths by Our Boots, who to that point had beaten Whirlaway in four of their five meetings. Worse, the Blue Grass was Whirlaway's first

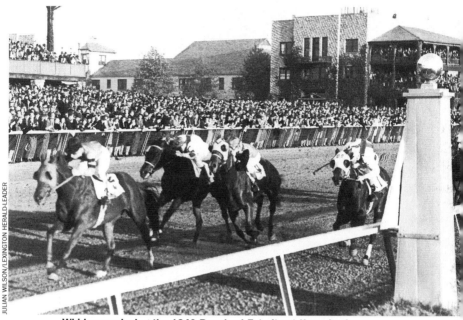

JULIAN WILSON/LEXINGTON HERALD-LEADER

**Whirlaway winning the 1940 Breeders' Futurity at Keeneland**

start beyond a mile and one-sixteenth, casting doubts on his ability to get the Derby distance. Then the colt ran second to Blue Pair in the Derby Trial on the Tuesday before the Derby, once again costing himself the race by bearing out.

Jones had a problem on his hands and knew it. His best exercise rider, "Pinky" Brown, had the strength and nerve to handle Whirlaway in his morning workouts and was devotedly attached to the colt, staying with him day and night. But Pinky (who got his nickname from his albino coloration) had poor vision, and there was no question of putting him on the colt's back under racing conditions even if he could make the weight. Wendell Eads, Calumet's contract jockey, had won with the colt but clearly lacked the muscle and balance to keep Whirly on a straight course. He may have been a little afraid of him as well.

Fortunately, a solution was available. Although America's leading jockey, Eddie Arcaro, was under contract to Greentree Stable, Greentree didn't have a Derby colt in 1941, leaving Arcaro free to accept an outside mount for the Derby. Arcaro had plenty of nerve as well as

strength, skill, and an almost uncanny ability to read a horse's mind and know what the animal might do. The only problem was the jockey's lack of enthusiasm about the prospect of riding Whirlaway. Jones had originally contacted him at the time Whirlaway left Florida, and at the time Arcaro had been noncommittal, partly because he didn't know that far in advance whether Greentree would have another riding assignment for him somewhere else on Derby day and partly because Arcaro wasn't at all sure he wanted any part of a colt that he privately considered to be more than a little crazy.

Mr. Longtail's long tail

Jones persisted, however, and when Arcaro mentioned Jones' request to Greentree trainer John Gaver, Gaver urged him to take the opportunity. Mostly swayed by Gaver's insistence that it would be foolish not to play ball with a master trainer who might have other good assignments to hand out, Arcaro finally agreed to take the Derby mount on Whirlaway even though he was less enthusiastic than ever after learning about the colt's performances in the Blue Grass and Derby Trial. By that time Whirlaway had been beaten on eight different racetracks by twenty different horses — not exactly a record to make him a rival of the greats of the past. There was no question that he had talent, but consistency was another matter.

Arcaro took his first ride on Whirlaway the day before the Derby. It was only a half-mile breeze but with a twist Arcaro hadn't quite

**Trainer Ben Jones aboard his headstrong champion**

BELMONT NEWS BUREAU

expected. As Arcaro waited for instructions for the workout, Jones planted himself about ten or twelve feet from the rail on the back of a fat stable pony and told Arcaro to ride Whirlaway through the hole. In his autobiography, *I Ride to Win*, Arcaro later confessed to having had his doubts about Jones' sanity, but as he said, "I figured if the old man was game enough to stand there, I was game enough to run him down." Arcaro sent Whirlaway at the hole and the colt ran straight and true, skimming the rail and passing the test easily.

Arcaro may not have known that following the Blue Grass Stakes Jones had been drilling the colt in similar fashion with Pinky Brown in the saddle, but during that single breeze Arcaro had quickly developed his own method for handling the unpredictable colt. "You had to take a long hold on him and freeze with it," he said later in *I Ride to Win*. "Although I might look like a coachman, it was the only way to handle him."

Jones got another idea while Pinky Brown was sending the colt through a ten-furlong workout the Monday of Derby week. Although

Pinky successfully kept the colt from bearing out, Whirlaway's stride chopped and bobbled, causing the exercise rider to wonder what was wrong with the colt. With his poor vision Pinky had not been able to see the shadows thrown by the inside rail — shadows the nervous Whirlaway had been jumping — but Jones had seen the problem and gotten a brainwave in the process. Distracted by the shadows he could see to his left, Whirlaway apparently hadn't even thought about trying to duck to his right. If the colt's vision could be restricted so that he could see much better to the left than to the right, might that not also keep him from bearing out?

Hence, the story that in the Derby saddling area Arcaro got another shock as Jones, muttering, "I'm gonna fix that son of a #$%^&," pulled out a knife. For a moment the jockey wondered if Jones meant to use it on Whirlaway, but the trainer merely used his blade to pare away the left cup of Whirlaway's blinkers. Thus was born Whirlaway's trademark one-eyed blinker, which allowed him unrestricted vision to the left while blocking his view to the right.

Actually, other accounts indicate that Jones made his alterations to the blinkers a few days before the Derby, which seems more reasonable although Arcaro himself later said the change was made on Derby day (though not with a knife in the saddling paddock!). Nor was it an unprecedented idea, as Jones had used similar equipment on another horse earlier in his training career. Nonetheless, it was the second major change for Whirlaway in a relatively short time, following the change of rider.

Whether the public knew about the equipment change or not, they did know Arcaro's ability, and Whirlaway was made the Derby favorite in spite of the fact that both of the colts that had so recently beaten him — Our Boots and Blue Pair — were in the Derby field. There were other challengers as well, most notably Porter's Cap, the Santa Anita Derby and Chesapeake Stakes winner and the second choice in the betting. Another well-regarded colt was Dispose, winner of the Flamingo Stakes that Whirlaway had skipped. Nearly lost in the shadows cast by more precocious colts was the late-developing Market

Wise, winner of the Wood Memorial at Jamaica and later a tough stayer and a champion in the handicap ranks.

Whirlaway was in peak condition for the Derby, his golden chestnut coat shining and dappled. The noisy Derby crowd at the saddling paddock presented a challenge for a horse of Whirlaway's disposition, but Ben Jones solved the problem by getting to the enclosure last of the entire field, with just enough time to slap the saddle on and throw Arcaro aboard before the call to the post. (Jones continued this pattern with his later Derby horses to avoid unnecessary wear and tear on their nerves in the paddock. His methods earned him complaints from his fellow trainers and the ire of the stewards, but as he said to racing writer John "Trader" Clark, "What's a one hundred-dollar fine when you are trying to win the Derby?")

There was no time for instructions, and no need for any; Arcaro had already been told the night before what not to do, which was to break Whirlaway sharply from the gate. Jones did not want the colt to take the lead before the field had straightened away in the homestretch, where Whirlaway would have a straight path to follow and be less likely to get disoriented. He also didn't want Whirlaway using his devastating turn of foot too early, for Whirlaway was not a horse who could come up with a second burst of speed; he had one tremendous run in him and that was it.

The race went just as Jones had hoped. Breaking sixth from the number four position in the field of eleven, Whirlaway was blocked in the first eighth of a mile and was taken back where Arcaro could drop him toward the rail and save ground.

With half the race run, Whirlaway was sixth and about nine lengths off of Dispose and Blue Pair, who were battling on the front end. At the mile Dispose was still hanging on gamely, having shaken off the fading Blue Pair, but Porter's Cap was at the leader's throat and Whirlaway was on the move from fourth, only two lengths off the lead. Splitting horses on the final turn, Whirlaway devoured the tiring leaders in a flash, with the California longshot Staretor and Market Wise close on his heels. Both ran with determined courage, but neither was any match for

Whirlaway. Running straight and true, his signature long tail flying behind, the little chestnut (he measured about 15.2 hands at the time of his Triple Crown campaign) uncorked a devastating finishing kick with a final quarter run in :23 4/5. He won by eight lengths over Staretor in track-record time of 2:01 2/5, two-fifths of a second faster than Twenty Grand's previous record from 1931. The time stood as a track record for twenty-one years before Decidedly flew the distance in 2:00 2/5 to win the 1962 Derby.

So impressive was Whirlaway's performance that some people did not believe it was talent alone that had propelled him. Rumors — apparently started by the trainer of a losing rival — were circulated after the Derby that Whirlaway had been under the influence of a stimulant, and the ordinarily calm Ben Jones was, for once, enraged at the innuendos. Churchill Downs officials, however, insisted publicly and loudly that the colt's post-race drug tests had been negative, and two weeks later Whirlaway proved his Derby performance had been no fluke by unleashing a similar burst of speed a half-mile out from the wire to win the Preakness by five and a half lengths.

Only three horses turned out to challenge Whirlaway for the Belmont Stakes three weeks later, and the number might have been lower still had Whirlaway, only days before the big race, not turned in a blistering workout that left some questions as to how much gas he might have in the tank for the race itself. Trying to blunt Whirly's famous finishing kick, his rivals attempted to set an artificially slow pace, but after a half-mile Arcaro was wise to the game and turned his colt loose. Whirlaway kicked clear by seven lengths, and though he won by a dwindling two and a half lengths in an unimpressive time of 2:31, he had done enough — "without drawing a deep breath," according to Arcaro — to win the Belmont and the Triple Crown with it.

Whirlaway went on to lock up Horse of the Year titles in 1941 and again in 1942, despite losing two of three races against Alsab, the champion three-year-old colt of 1942. Whirlaway was also voted champion three-year-old male in 1941 and champion handicap male in 1942. The first horse to pass the $500,000 mark in earnings, Whirlaway retired

## Kentucky Derby
## Purse: $75,000 Added

7th Race  Churchill Downs - May 3, 1941. Sixty-seventh running Kentucky Derby
Purse $75,000 added. Three-year-olds. 1 1-4 Miles. Main Track. Track: Fast.
Net value to winner, $61,275 and gold trophy; second, $8,000; third, $3,000; fourth, $1,000.

| Horse | A | Wgt | Eqp | Odds | PP | St | 1/2 | 3/4 | 1 | Str | Fin | Jockey |
|---|---|---|---|---|---|---|---|---|---|---|---|---|
| Whirlaway | 3 | 126 | wb | 2.90 | 4 | 6 | $8^1$ | $6^{1\frac{1}{2}}$ | $4^1$ | $1^3$ | $1^8$ | E Arcaro |
| Staretor | 3 | 126 | w | 36.00 | 2 | 1 | $7^2$ | $4^{1\frac{1}{2}}$ | $5^3$ | $2^{\frac{1}{2}}$ | $2^{nk}$ | G Woolf |
| Market Wise | 3 | 126 | wb | 19.10 | 7 | 5 | $6^2$ | $8^4$ | $6^3$ | $5^3$ | $3^2$ | I Anderson |
| Porter's Cap | 3 | 126 | wb | 3.30 | 9 | 4 | $2^h$ | $3^5$ | $2^{1\frac{1}{2}}$ | $3^h$ | $4^1$ | L Haas |
| Little Beans | 3 | 126 | wb | 12.10 | 5 | 10 | $10^{12}$ | $9^8$ | $8^5$ | $7^2$ | $5^1$ | G Moore |
| Dispose | 3 | 126 | w | 7.20 | 11 | 2 | $1^2$ | $1^2$ | $1^h$ | $4^h$ | $6^{1\frac{1}{2}}$ | C Bierman |
| Blue Pair | 3 | 126 | wb | 20.60 | 3 | 3 | $3^5$ | $2^h$ | $3^{\frac{1}{2}}$ | $6^{\frac{1}{2}}$ | $7^{\frac{1}{2}}$ | B James |
| Our Boots | 3 | 126 | w | 3.90 | 10 | 9 | $4^3$ | $5^{\frac{1}{2}}$ | $7^2$ | $8^5$ | $8^3$ | C McCreary |
| Robert Morris | 3 | 126 | w | 13.90 | 8 | 8 | $5^{1\frac{1}{2}}$ | $7^1$ | $9^6$ | $9^8$ | $9^{12}$ | H Richards |
| Valdina Paul | 3 | 126 | wb | †24.30 | 6 | 7 | $9^3$ | $10^{15}$ | $10^{15}$ | $10^{15}$ | $10^{12}$ | H Lemmons |
| Swain | 3 | 126 | wb | † | 1 | 11 | 11 | 11 | 11 | 11 | 11 | J Adams |

† Mutuel field.

**Off Time:** 5:55  **Time Of Race:** :23¾  :46½  1:11½  1:37½  2:01¼ (new track record).
**Start:** Good and slow  **Track:** Fast
**Equipment::** w for whip; b for blinkers

**Mutuel Payoffs**

| 4 | Whirlaway | $7.80 | $5.00 | $4.40 |
|---|---|---|---|---|
| 2 | Staretor | | 35.20 | 17.00 |
| 7 | Market Wise | | | 10.80 |

**Winner:**  Whirlaway, ch. c. by Blenheim II—Dustwhirl, by Sweep (Trained by B. A. Jones).
Bred by Calumet Farm in Ky.

**Start good and slow. Won easily; second and third driving.**

WHIRLAWAY, eased back when blocked in the first eighth and taken to the inside approaching the first turn, started up after reaching the final half-mile, was taken between horses on the final turn, responded with much energy to take command with a rush and, continuing with much power, drew out fast in the final eighth. STARETOR, away slowly and allowed to remain well back the first five-eighths, made his move gradually, drifted out slightly before straightening up in the stretch and held on well in the final drive. MARKET WISE, also well back early, was slow to respond to pressure, but rallied after reaching the last five-sixteenths and, finishing with courage, was wearing down STARETOR. PORTER'S CAP, a strong factor from the start and always clear as he raced on the outside, responded to strong urging when rounding the final turn, but tired after reaching the last three-sixteenths. LITTLE BEANS raced well from a very sluggish beginning, then closed courageously to pass tired horses in the stretch. DISPOSE took command easily, was allowed to run along well within himself through the backstretch, was under pressure after three-quarters and held on fairly well to the closing three-sixteenths, where he faltered badly. BLUE PAIR quit after showing speed for a mile. OUR BOOTS could not go with the early leaders under urging and failed to keep up after reaching the last half-mile. ROBERT MORRIS began well, but dropped out of contention after a half-mile and was far back thereafter.

**Owners:**  (1) Calumet Farm; (2) H S Nesbitt; (3) L Tufano; (4) C S Howard; (5) Mrs L Palladino; (6) King Ranch; (7) Mrs V S Bragg; (8) Woodvale Farm; (9) J F Byers; (10) Valdina Farm; (11) C Putnam

after two unsuccessful starts at age five with a record of thirty-two wins, fifteen seconds, and nine thirds from sixty starts. He had won races from five furlongs to two miles and had successfully carried up to 130 pounds.

Whirlaway made his final public appearance under colors at Washington Park on July 5, 1943, with Pinky Brown in the saddle for the exhibition. He then shipped home to Calumet to take up stud duties alongside a young stallion named Bull Lea, whose first foals were three-year-olds in 1944. Given the pick of Calumet's mares at first, Whirlaway eventually sired eighteen stakes winners, including 1948 Coaching Club American Oaks winner Scattered, but was rapidly overshadowed by Bull Lea, whose first crop included 1944 Horse of the Year Twilight Tear and 1947 Horse of the Year Armed. Bull Lea would go on to earn five titles as leading sire in the United States, and it was no secret that Ben Jones favored the durable, good-natured horses that Bull Lea turned out so consistently over the more physically and mentally erratic stock sired by Whirlaway.

Although Whirlaway was only twelve at the time, his best days at stud were already behind him when the famed French breeder Marcel Boussac leased him in 1950. (Boussac later bought the horse outright.) The expatriated stallion sired nothing of any note in his adopted country. Whirlaway died in France on April 6, 1953, ten minutes after breeding his last mare. The cause of death was apparently a heart attack. He was buried in France, but a marker was erected in his memory in Calumet Farm's famous horse cemetery and can still be seen at the farm. A memorial of another sort exists at the National Museum of Racing's Hall of Fame, where Whirlaway joined the roster of American racing's greats in 1959.

None of Whirlaway's sons were of any account as stallions, and his primary legacy in Thoroughbred breeding is through his daughter Rock Drill, whose daughter Lady Pitt was both the champion three-year-old filly of 1966 and a notable broodmare whose family is still going strong. Some of Whirlaway's electric burst of speed may also have passed through his daughter Scattered, whose great-great-grandson Dash for Cash was twice the world's champion racing Quarter Horse and proved a great sire in that breed. But the primary legacy of Whirlaway has been in memory, of a horse whose personality was as remarkable as his talent. If his quirks kept him from being numbered among the greatest of the great, they also endeared him to millions of fans and made him the horse that kept a generation of racegoers at the edge of its seat. Few have done more.

*By Avalyn Hunter*

# The Unlikeliest of Heroes
## (Rich Strike, 2022)

THE KENTUCKY DERBY IS the most scrutinized, analyzed, and publicized horse race in America. When the horses get in the starting gate, racing fans and bettors already know pretty much everything there is to know about them. But in 2022 when a chestnut colt with red and white silks and red blinkers came charging through along the inside and crossed the finish line three-quarters of a length ahead of the favorite, Epicenter, hardly anyone had a clue who he was. The only reason they would know the name Rich Strike was from seeing it on his Derby saddlecloth that he wore in the morning despite still needing several horses to drop out in order to make it into the starting field of twenty.

Even the day before the Derby very few had ever heard of the horse, having paid little attention to him all the time he had been on the also-eligible list. Now here he was not only an eleventh-hour addition to the Derby field, but winning the race at odds of 80-1, the second biggest longshot winner in history behind Donerail's 91-1 odds in 1913.

But who was he? Not since the Venezuelan invader Canonero II in 1971 had a horse won the Derby with so little known about him. And this was a horse bred by the one-time powerhouse Calumet Farm.

If you had looked up the history of Rich Strike you would have seen that his dam, Gold Strike, had sold for a paltry $1,700 as a weanling and that he had been claimed in his second start for $30,000 by small-time trainer Eric Reed.

"It's crazy, isn't it; you can't make this stuff up," said Tommy Wente, who bought Gold Strike for practically nothing. "I'm a cheap buyer. My clients and I can't afford the big prices. I loved this mare, even though I knew she had problems getting in foal since producing her Keen Ice colt [later to be named Rich Strike]. And I knew Calumet Farm wanted to get rid of her as they often do with older mares. I just thought I would take a shot. I bought her for M. C. Roberts, who has a farm in Indiana. He took great care of her, but he couldn't get her in foal. Finally, he called me and said, 'I'm done. I'm at my wit's end.' I suggested he send her to a specialist to try to find out why she couldn't get in foal, but he kept insisting he was done, so he gave her away to Austin Nicks, who has a farm in Sellersburg, Indiana. A week after he gave her away her son won the Kentucky Derby. I'm telling you, you can't make this stuff up."

So from a family inundated with cheap claimers over the years, a number of runners from small Canadian tracks, and a mare who was given away a week before her son won the Derby came one of the great stories in the annals of the Kentucky Derby and one of its most shocking winners ever.

But let's begin the story on September 21, 2021. Eric Reed had put a claim in on a horse at Churchill Downs, but there were seven or eight claims in the box and he lost the shake. So he decided to claim another horse later on the card who had run once on the grass at Ellis Park, finishing tenth, beaten by fourteen lengths, but this race was on the dirt. This time, with the horse having run so poorly in his debut, Reed's was the only claim and he was able to take over the training of a chestnut colt named Rich Strike, who wound up winning that race by a staggering seventeen and a quarter lengths.

After sending Rich Strike, who they nicknamed "Richie," to Fair Grounds, Reed put Venezuelan-born jockey Sonny Leon on the colt, but in his first start, the Gun Runner Stakes, he ran poorly. It turned out he was very anemic after the race and was found to be suffering from stomach ulcers. After he finished third in the Leonatus Stakes and closed from eleventh to finish fourth, beaten three by lengths, in the John Battaglia, Leon dismounted and told Reed, "We're there. This is a Derby horse." The ulcers fully cleared up by the time of the rich Jeff Ruby Steaks and when Reed's veterinarian Alan Dorton saw the move Rich Strike made, closing from eleventh to finish third at 26-1, he thought, "This horse actually could win the Derby if he gets in or at least surprise a lot of people. If he had another eighth of a mile I believe he would have won that race."

But Rich Strike had a mischievous streak in him. The colt liked to play with his water bucket and a month before the Derby, as he had done before, he cut his nose open on the bucket and Dorton had to sew it up. "Here it is a month before the Derby and I'm sewing his nose up," Dorton said. "I used pink stitches and told people on Facebook to keep an eye out for those pink stitches because they might be at Churchill Downs. We did blood work on him before the Derby and it came back great. I told Eric 'We're in good shape.' That's when everyone started feeling he could win if he got in."

Reed's daughter Lindsy, who is a top hunter jumper, began taking care of Rich Strike, grooming him, bandaging him, and giving him his medicines, and would until he left for Churchill Downs to prepare for a possible start in the Derby.

"He was quite full of himself and could be a handful," she said. "He would rear up and was just playful and kind of goofy like a young prankster growing up. If you left him alone he was fine, but if you bothered him he'd eat you alive. He really wasn't mean, he loved to play with his grooms."

In the weeks leading up to the Derby, Eric Reed and his team just waited and hoped for a chance to get into the starting field, believing they had a better horse who was capable of running a better race than everyone thought.

Two weeks before the Derby jockey and exercise rider Gabriel Lagunes' alarm clock went off at 4:00 a.m. By 4:30 he was out of his house in Florence, Kentucky and on the road for the two-hour drive to Churchill Downs. The Mexican-born jockey was on a special assignment. Eric Reed, for whom Lagunes began riding at Mountaineer Park

**Rich Strike walking on the track during morning workout on
Wednesday, May 4, 2022, as he prepared for the
148th running of the Kentucky Derby at Churchill Downs.**

two years earlier and exercised horses at Turfway Park, had asked his
rider to drive to Churchill Downs every morning to get on Rich Strike,
who had run three times over Turfway's synthetic surface. He hardly
seemed like Kentucky Derby material, but he had enough points to at
least have him placed at number 24 on the earnings list. And it was

obvious the colt, who came from far back in his races, was getting good at the right time, so why not train him at Churchill and see what happened, even though getting him in the race seemed like a longshot.

There was no one Reed wanted on the colt's back other than Lagunes. The previous November at Turfway Park, Reed told Lagunes "I need you to work with this horse and take care of him," so he started exercising the colt and working with him. And boy was he a handful.

"He was kind of goofy, he had his problems and needed a lot of work," said Lagunes, who was a top jockey in Mexico and once finished second in the rich Clasico del Caribe in Puerto Rico. "He was sore in his back and ankles, he was very green and was mean in the mornings, he was scared of other horses behind him and in front of him, and he didn't like ponies. He just didn't want horses close to him. Every morning we would ice him and I would walk him and talk to him and jog him to try to get him to relax. I would gallop him way out in the middle of the track because he was so strong and if I got him close to the rail he would know he was working and would be hard to hold.

"We raced him in blinkers, but he seemed nervous in them so I suggested to Eric that he open up the blinkers and use cheaters because he needed to see everything and that would relax him more."

Rich Strike had changed quite a bit since he was broken by April Mayberry in Ocala, Florida. "He was just one of the boys back then," she said. "He was young like a teenager and his mind was never really in it. He was always messing around and playing. But he learned and became a very game and confident colt. I'm surprised to hear they had problems with him, but when I had him he was still a baby."

Everyone on Reed's team knew the chances of getting in the Derby were slim, but they remained hopeful, believing he could run well because of his running style, his late closing punch, and how quickly he was improving. When Reed told Lindsy about their plans to try to get in the Derby she was "amazed and excited," mostly for her father and mother to have this opportunity. She never thought he would win, but it was exciting just to be able to get there.

On April 27, Lagunes worked him five furlongs at Churchill Downs and he went in a sharp :59 3/5.

"I could feel he was getting better and better the last few weeks and he was so strong in his work and really happy," Lagunes said.

But as the Derby got closer the chances of Rich Strike getting in grew slimmer. Reed had someone giving him information every day about the status of the field and he would text him whenever a horse withdrew. There was some hope when he jumped from twenty-fourth on the list to twenty-second, but after the Lexington Stakes they were back to twenty-four. All they could do now was enter the horse and put him on the also-eligible list, hoping somehow four horses would drop out.

"We came here on a prayer," Reed said. "I told my dad and I told Rick [owner Richard Dawson], the worst thing that could happen to us is to have a call a day or two before the Derby and say you're going to get in and not be prepared. So we came up to Churchill and we trained against all odds. Nobody thought we could get in. We got a defection, and then we got another one."

But they still needed another one and there was nothing left to do but wait and hope for a last-minute miracle. Reed's wife Kay kept calling Lindsy to find out what was happening and the question everyone kept asking her was, "Any word? Any word?"

At 8:45 the morning before the Derby, Reed was notified that there were no scratches and that they were not going to get in. The security guard assigned to the colt was told to leave the barn and Reed texted his dad and simply said, "Didn't happen." He texted some of his friends and said, "We didn't get in. Sorry guys." He then went in to his crew to tell them in person because he knew they were going to be really let down. "I told them, 'Guys, look, we didn't make it, but we were Number Twenty-One.'" They were one spot away from experiencing the moment of their lives, but time was desperately running out and it seemed hopeless.

Reed told his crew, "We got to get ready for the Peter Pan [at Belmont Park] next week. And if we run well, we'll go to the Belmont and show them that we belong."

"I was trying to keep their spirits up," Reed said. "It didn't matter how I felt because I have to keep my crew going. And they were really sad."

Then just before nine o'clock, Reed's pony girl Fifi called him and said "Don't do anything with your horse. Don't move him."

Reed had no idea what she was talking about and said, "What do you mean? Calm down." But she was still excited. "No, you're getting in," she said. But Reed still didn't believe her. "No I'm not. I've already been told I'm not. Somebody gave you bad information," he said.

But Fifi insisted. "I'm telling you I just got notification that Wayne [Lukas] is scratching [Ethereal Road] and you're going to get in."

Shortly after, Reed received a call from steward Barbara Borden who said, "This is the steward. Tomorrow in the twelfth race, the Kentucky Derby, do you want to draw in off the also eligible?"

"I couldn't even breathe to answer and say 'yes,'" Reed said. "I was like, what just happened? I was told no I'm not in, I lost my security guard, and now we're in."

Lindsy finally got to tell everyone, "Well boys, he's in the Derby." She called Dorton and said, "We got in; cross your fingers."

Were the Derby gods at work conjuring up this unlikely scenario? The Reeds had gone through a number of tragedies and nearly left the business. But they proved how strong the human spirit was, especially through the incredible bond that has held the family together.

In December 2017, the Reeds lost twenty-three horses in a fire at his farm, the Mercury Equine Center outside Lexington, Kentucky. Reed told Kay, "We've probably lost everything." But as he said, by the grace of God the wind was blowing in the direction where it prevented the fire from spreading to his other two barns. But his entire operation was nearly wiped out. In addition to the horses, they lost all their tack and supplies along with valuable records, trophies, and racing memorabilia. It pretty much destroyed their past existence that had taken so many years to build up. Fortunately, owner and breeder Ken Ramsey sent them twenty-two horses to help get them back on their feet. He also had his veterinarian Alan Dorton go there to help take care of the horses and they have remained close ever since.

The Reeds built back their operation, but the tragedies were far from over. In the summer of 2020 Eric Reed's two main assistants, behind Kay, James Wellman and Hollywood Sweeney, who had been with him for more than twenty-five years, both died of cancer several months apart. Lindsy would like to believe it was James and Hollywood who helped clear a path for Rich Strike, one on the inside and one on the outside, as he made his epic charge through the Derby field.

They had suffered though the ordeal of the fire, but were unable to rejoice in the victory of a lifetime. "The last thing they would remember was the fire, watching the barn burn down and the bodies being taken out," Lindsy said.

Shortly after losing James and Hollywood, the Reeds' daughter Jessica (the second oldest of four children) and her two-year-old son Raylin were visiting Jessica's husband at the garage where he worked when there was a tragic accident that killed Raylin. Her husband still hasn't recovered.

"The father has been dealing with serious psychological issues since," said Alan Dorton.

After having to suffer through that terrible tragedy Kay lost both her parents a short time later. But through all the heartbreak, the family held together and kept forging ahead, looking for that one big horse.

They found him in the unlikeliest way and now here they were in the Kentucky Derby. How they got there was amazing in itself.

Going to the paddock before the race Eric Reed was happy to see Rich Strike calm and handling everything like a pro, just as he done all week schooling. When he got to the paddock he was composed and nothing seemed to bother him. Once he got on the track he perked up, yet was still well behaved.

On the tote board he was 80-1, with no one paying any attention to him, especially getting into the race the day before and having done little of note in his races. He was considered merely a last-minute throw-in who really didn't belong in the race. Although he had to break from post twenty, Sonny Leon was able to work out a trip and get him to the rail, where he has always loved to be. On the far turn Reed lost him for a second, then saw him cut to the inside. "That's when I almost passed out," he said. "I didn't remember what happened after that."

Somehow the seas had parted and Leon and Rich Strike were able to weave their way through the field. Down the stretch following a blazing fast pace of :21 3/5 and :45 1/5, the favored Epicenter took over the lead as the pacesetters wilted badly from the fast early fractions. Then Zandon came charging at him and it looked like a two-horse battle to the wire. Epicenter dug in and refused to let Zandon get by him and appeared to have the race won. Just then another horse came flying up the rail, eased outside of a tiring Messier, and stormed up inside the two leaders. Most people had no idea who it was. Even track announcer Travis Stone and NBC race caller Larry Collmus missed him, not mentioning his name until he came charging by Epicenter and Zandon. He already had his head in front when Collmus realized who it was and shouted, "Oh my goodness!"

**Rich Strike, ridden by Sonny Leon, winning the Kentucky Derby on May 7, 2022.**

Even April Mayberry, watching in her living room with her mother, her assistant trainer, and several friends, didn't recognize him. "I saw it was a chestnut and thought it was Taiba," she said. "But then I saw the blinkers and thought 'You got to be kidding, it's Rich Strike.' When he crossed the finish line everyone went so crazy my poor dogs ran out of the house. I thought the neighbors were going to call the police."

In the paddock, Gabriel Lagunes and his partner Lindsey Matthews watched along with the Reeds. "We were completely shocked," Lindsey said. "This was not what we were expecting. We were all jumping up and down and there was lots of crying and hugging. It looked like Eric was having a heart attack."

Lindsy Reed said hugging her father and grandfather was "the greatest moment I will ever remember. We wrapped our arms around each other in total astonishment. I wanted this so much for my dad and mom. It's been a hard road and they really deserve this. I just wanted him to get in the race for them. I never thought he had a chance to win, but he proved me wrong in the biggest way possible. I was so happy he at least got to run, but he blew us out of the ballpark."

**Rich Strike with jockey Sonny Leon at the 148th running of the Kentucky Derby.**

Owner Richard Dawson said after the race, "What planet is this? I feel like I've been propelled somewhere." He asked Reed, "Are you sure this isn't a dream?"

All the work and all the anxiety of trying to get in the Derby had paid off in shocking fashion. Rich Strike no longer was that baby whose mind was more interested in "messing around and playing." He no longer was that "goofy" colt with all the hang-ups who was afraid of other horses.

But it was obvious he still was the same colt who disliked ponies, as witnessed by his constant attempts to savage the lead pony escorting him to the winner's circle. Meanwhile, in the grandstand and infield most everyone was savaging their mutuel tickets, wondering what had just happened.

So we came to the end of another Kentucky Derby journey. Somehow the Derby gods worked their miracle, as they have done a number of times in the past. The unlikeliest of heroes, Rich Strike,

JOHN SOMMERS II / UPI / ALAMY LIVE NEWS

**Rich Strike owner Richard Dawson (right), trainer Eric Reed (center), and jockey Sonny Leon (left) in the winner's circle after the 148th running of the Kentucky Derby at Churchill Downs on Saturday, May 7, 2022.**

struck it rich and added a wild new chapter into the annals of the Kentucky Derby. It sure didn't end like we expected, but that is what the Derby trail and the Derby itself is all about. Always expect the unexpected, because you never know whose dreams are destined to come true. In this case even the dreamers couldn't imagine they would come true. But in the end, the Derby gods spoke, and when they speak the whole world listens.

"We had a lot of people watching over us," Lindsy said. "It was as if it was meant to be. It was like, 'You've been through so much and lost so much maybe a miracle can come your way.' God has mysterious ways of working. He gave us 'Richie' and it was up to us to put the pieces of the puzzle together. A little bit of faith can move mountains . . . and it did."

*By Steve Haskin*

# Authors / Panelists

## AUTHORS

**Edward L. Bowen** is the award-winning author of more than twenty books on Thoroughbred racing history, including biographies of Man o' War and War Admiral and a two-volume set on the great breeders, entitled *Legacies of the Turf*. Bowen lives in Versailles, Kentucky.

**Timothy T. Capps** was the author of the Thoroughbred Legends books on Secretariat, Spectacular Bid, and Affirmed and Alydar. He served as executive director of the Maryland Jockey Club and as editor and publisher of *MidAtlantic Thoroughbred*. Capps lived in Columbia, Maryland.

**Tracy Gantz** has served as managing editor of John Lyons' *Perfect Horse* magazine, *The Thoroughbred of California*, and *Paint Horse Journal*. She began her career at *The Blood-Horse*, where she is the southern California correspondent, and also was the West Coast breeding columnist for *Daily Racing Form*. She lives in the San Gabriel Valley of the Los Angeles area.

**Evan I. Hammonds** was managing editor of *The Blood-Horse* from 1998 to 2020, and editorial director from 2020 to 2021. He previously worked as an editor for Daily Racing Form in Hightstown, New Jersey, and in Phoenix, Arizona, and was the Midlantic edition editor of *Figs Form* in New York City. He lives in Versailles, Kentucky.

**Craig Harzmann** is a freelance racing journalist and sixth-grade teacher. In addition to being the southern California correspondent for The Blood-Horse, he has written for many industry publications, including *California Thoroughbred* and *Paddock*. He lives in Lake View Terrace, California.

**Steve Haskin** has been national correspondent for *Daily Racing Form* and senior correspondent for *The Blood-Horse* and provided lead coverage of the Triple Crown for over twenty years; he now covers the Triple Crown for Secretariat.com. He is the author of multiple books, including *Horse Racing's Holy Grail: The Epic Quest for the Kentucky Derby*. He lives in Rocky Hill, Connecticut.

**Avalyn Hunter** is a nationally recognized authority on Thoroughbred pedigrees and racing history whose work has appeared in publications such as *The Blood-Horse*, *Thoroughbred Times*, and *Louisiana Horse*. She is the author of several books, including *American Classic Pedigrees*. She lives in Lake City, Florida.

**Robert Kieckhefer** is vice president for public affairs for Blue Cross/Blue Shield and an Illinois correspondent for *The Blood-Horse*. He lives in Oak Park, Illinois.

**Eliza R.L. McGraw** is a freelance writer living in Washington, D.C. Her work has appeared in *The Blood-Horse*, *EQUUS*, and *The Washington Post*. She is the author of *Everyday Horsemanship* and *Here Comes Exterminator!*

**Gary McMillen** is the former assistant director of human resources at Louisiana State University Health Sciences Center. He has served as the New Orleans correspondent for *The Blood-Horse*, written for *Louisiana Horse* magazine, and provided a weekly feature for Fair Grounds' website. He lives in New Orleans.

## PANELISTS

**Bob Adair** served as assistant sports editor and/or sports editor for both the Lexington *Herald* and Lexington *Leader* from 1942 to 1957. He covered racing and served as assistant sports editor for the Louisville *Courier-Journal* from 1957 to 1985.

**Mike Battaglia** was the "voice of Churchill Downs" from the late 1970s to 1996 and is currently the track handicapper and analyst for Churchill Downs. His first Derby call? The epic Affirmed/Alydar meeting in 1978.

**Steve Haskin** (See biography in the "Authors" section.)

For four decades **Joe Hirsch**, *Daily Racing Form's* legendary executive columnist, kept the racing world abreast of the comings and goings of the sport through his outstanding journalism. His "Derby Doings" was a must-read in the weeks leading up to the Derby. Hirsch, who retired in 2003, is the author or co-author of five books.

**Jim McKay**, the long-time sports journalist for ABC Sports, covered every sport under the sun for "Wide World of Sports," including the Kentucky Derby. Prior to his work with ABC, McKay's work with CBS also included coverage of horse racing.